1 Introduction
The uncertain promise of Chinese science

'By the end of 2020… China will achieve more science and technological breakthroughs of great world influence, qualifying it to join the ranks of the world's most innovative countries.'

President Hu Jintao, 9 Jan 2006

The head office of Sibiono Genetech is nothing special to look at. An anonymous blend of grey and glass, it is just another business unit, one of thousands that can be found in the science parks that now fringe the outskirts of China's larger cities.

What lies inside is more unusual. Sibiono's elite team of biochemists are in the frontline of the war against cancer. In 2003, they received regulatory approval for the world's first gene therapy treatment. Known as Gendicine, this pioneering drug was developed to combat head and neck tumours. Results so far look promising: patients receiving a combination of Gendicine and radiotherapy show three times more tumour regression than those receiving radiotherapy alone. Survival rates after three years are 14 per cent higher.[1] Dr Dinggang Li, a surgical oncologist at Beijing's Haidian Hospital, has used it on more than 250 patients, and describes it as 'a milestone on the order of penicillin'.[2]

The potential of gene therapy has long excited cancer researchers. But international opinion about Gendicine remains divided. Some see it as a sign of the growing strength of Chinese biomedicine, and predict many more breakthroughs to come. 'If I were making a long-term investment in biotech, and particularly in gene therapy', says James Norris, Professor of Microbiology at the Medical University of South Carolina, 'I would be making it in China, not here.'[3] Others are more sceptical, raising questions about the reliability of the clinical trial data and the permissiveness of Beijing's drug regulations. Detailed data on Gendicine has been published only in Chinese language journals, and Marshall Posner, an associate professor at Harvard Medical School, complains that Sibiono has 'not yet released any data in an internationally accessible, peer-reviewed journal that would allow objective analysis'.[4]

20%

Since 1999, China's spending on R&D has increased by more than 20 per cent each year.

In many ways, Sibiono Genetech represents the best of Chinese science. It has scored a global first in a complex field which is likely to grow exponentially. And in a country where the public sector still dominates scientific research, it is a rare commercial success story. Yet while Gendicine exemplifies China's innovative potential, it simultaneously raises questions about the governance and regulation of research, and the capacity of a Chinese start-up to outpace the giants of global biotechnology. It can be hard to see clearly through the clouds of hope, hype, promise and uncertainty that swirl around Gendicine. These same clouds hover over much of Chinese science.

From imitation to innovation

China in 2007 is the world's largest technocracy: a country ruled by scientists and engineers who believe in the power of new technologies to deliver social and economic progress. The Chinese science and innovation system has its weaknesses but one thing it excels at is the rapid mobilisation of resources. Right now, the country is at an early stage in the most ambitious programme of research investment since John F Kennedy embarked on the moon race.

The headline numbers are enough to make anyone pause for thought. Since 1999, China's spending on research and development (R&D) has increased by more than 20 per cent each year. In 2005, it reached 1.3 per cent of gross domestic product (GDP), up from 0.7 per cent in 1998. In December 2006, the Organisation for Economic Co-operation and Development (OECD) surprised policy-makers by announcing that China had moved ahead of Japan for the first time, to become the world's second highest R&D investor after the US.[5] Spending by central government in 2006 reached 71.6 billion RMB, or £4.7 billion, compared with £3.2 billion by the UK government. Meanwhile, countries across Europe are struggling to make headway towards the Lisbon targets of 3 per cent of GDP. Janez Potocnik,

Contents

First published in 2007
© Demos
Some rights reserved – see copyright licence for details

Series edited by Charles Leadbeater and James Wilsdon

ISBN 1 84180 173 9
Copy edited by Julie Pickard, London
Design by Browns (www.brownsdesign.com)
Printed by The Good News Press

For further information and subscription details please contact:
Demos, Magdalen House, 136 Tooley Street, London, SE1 2TU
telephone: 0845 458 5949 email: hello@demos.co.uk
web: www.demos.co.uk

the EU's research commissioner, admits: 'The Chinese trend is extremely clear... They will catch us up in 2009 or 2010.'[6]

It is when you roll these numbers forward that the sheer scale of what is under way becomes more apparent. In January 2006, China's Science and Technology Congress met for three days to approve a new Medium to Long Term Science and Technology Development Programme. This identifies priorities for the next 15 years and confirms the aim of boosting investment to 2 per cent of GDP by 2010 and 2.5 per cent by 2020. Reaching these targets will require investment in 2020 to be six times what it is today (see table 1).[7] The plan says that advances in science and technology should eventually account for 60 per cent of economic growth, and that China should aim to be among the top five countries worldwide in terms of patents and scientific citations. In his keynote speech to the Congress on 9 January 2006, President Hu Jintao called on China to become an 'innovation-oriented society'.[8]

Table 1 R&D spending targets in the Medium to Long-Term Plan

Year	R&D spending (all sources, US$ billions)	% of GDP	Central government (US$ billions)
2004	24.6	1.23	8.7
2010	45.0	2.00	18.0
2020	113.0	2.50	not known

Source: Adapted from 'China bets big on big science', *Science* 311, 17 Mar 2006.

China's long boom, in which growth has averaged 9 per cent a year for over a decade, has been propelled by a combination of low-cost manufacturing, imported technology and substantial flows of foreign investment. Such is the success of this model that China now produces 70 per cent of the world's photocopiers, 55 per cent of its DVD players and 25 per cent of its washing machines. But the new 15-year plan starts by acknowledging that while manufacturing remains crucial, it will not be sufficient to carry China through the next stage in its development. The plan mentions a series of 'acute challenges', including the availability of energy and resources, levels of environmental pollution, and weak capabilities for innovation. These can be overcome only through a new focus on 'independent innovation' (*zizhu chuangxin*).

Certain slogans and concepts have defined different periods in China's history: 'serve the people' in Mao's time; 'reform and opening' and 'the four modernisations' during the Deng Xiaoping period; 'the three represents' of Jiang Zemin; and under Hu Jintao phrases like 'the peaceful rise' and 'the harmonious society'. *Zizhu chuangxin* looks set to become another period-defining mantra. Policy-makers have decided that independent innovation is what China needs. It is no longer enough to import or copy high-end technologies from the US and Europe. If China is to find the place it wants in the world economy it needs to create its own technologies that can support future waves of economic growth.

The new plan goes on to describe the revolutionary potential of fields such as biotechnology and nanotechnology, and notes that many other countries are increasing their research budgets to meet these opportunities. 'Faced with the new international situation', it argues:

we must heighten our sense of responsibility and urgency; act more consciously and steadfastly to make S&T [science and technology] progress a primary driving force in economic and social development; regard the improvement of independent innovative capabilities as the centrepiece of our efforts to adjust our economic structure; change our growth mode, and improve the country's competitiveness; and view the construction of an innovative country as a future-oriented major strategic choice.[9]

Big plans

The Medium to Long-Term Plan includes the following elements:
— 68 priority goals spread across 11 key areas of importance to China's economy and development (eg energy, environment, agriculture, manufacturing, transport, public health)
— 16 special research projects, eg 'core electronic devices'; 'extremely large-scale integrated circuit manufacturing technologies'; 'wideband wireless mobile communications technology'; 'breed new transgenic biological varieties', 'large-scale advanced pressured-water reactor'; 'prevention of infectious diseases such as AIDS and hepatitis'; 'R&D of giant planes'; and 'manned space flights'
— eight 'cutting-edge' technology areas: biotech, IT, new materials, advanced manufacturing, advanced energy, marine technologies, lasers and aerospace
— eight 'cutting edge' science challenges, including in cognitive science, deep structure of matter, pure mathematics, earth systems science
— four major new research programmes in protein research, nanoscience, growth and reproduction, and quantum modulation research.

New measures being introduced to pursue these goals include:
— increasing R&D expenditure on science from 1.3 per cent of GDP to 2 per cent in 2010 and 2.5 per cent in 2020
— combining and coordinating military and civilian research organisations and the management of these
— new banking policies and fiscal incentives to support innovative start-ups, and greater investment in R&D by established firms
— introducing a new evaluation system for benchmarking research institutes and researchers
— a new national strategy on intellectual property rights.

Ready for take-off?
Drafting the new plan was a serious project in itself. Two thousand scientists spent three years debating the proposals, with the final decisions referred to a committee chaired by Prime Minister Wen Jiabao. The plan was presented as the most significant for several decades, and implicit parallels were drawn with its 1956 forerunner, which created many of China's research institutions and gave rise to its first atom bomb and satellite.

Like many such documents, the plan is long on aspiration and short on specifics.[10] But to what extent does it represent a landmark in Chinese policy? Seasoned observers stress the need to place the plan in the context of a wider set of reforms to the Chinese innovation system that are now reaching a tipping point. Denis Simon, a US expert with 25 years' experience of these debates, says:

It is clear to me that China has entered an important watershed period in terms of the operation and performance of its science and technology system... [It] is positioned for an important take-off – the question is no longer if this will happen but rather when.[11]

Simon offers four reasons for this upbeat assessment. First, Chinese policy is becoming more sophisticated and outward facing, as the government starts to think in terms of an integrated national system of innovation. Second, traditional forms of state planning and control are being replaced by lighter-touch, enabling frameworks, including new funding structures and performance measures, and a far greater role for enterprise and private sector R&D. Third, there has been a marked improvement in the university sector, both in terms of the quantity of graduates, with around 350,000 IT graduates in 2004, and also the quality of degrees and PhDs. Finally, China has stepped up the internationalisation of its research system, with extensive networks of collaboration across Europe, Japan and the US, and a more visible presence in international journals and conferences.

Yet despite progress across all of these fronts, it would be wrong to underplay the challenges that China must confront as it seeks to become an 'innovation-oriented society'. Richard P Suttmeier, professor of political science at the University of Oregon, is another veteran of these debates. Borrowing from Dickens, he suggests that Chinese science is experiencing 'the best of times and the worst of times'.[12] Contrary to notions of a technological juggernaut, the Chinese system suffers from several structural vulnerabilities, the greatest of which is what he terms the 'technology trap'. So much of China's growth and development has relied on imported technologies that only 0.03 per cent of Chinese firms own the intellectual property rights of the core technologies they use. This acts as a serious constraint on profitability. Universities and research institutes are becoming more productive, but Chinese enterprises still lag behind in terms of R&D intensity and patenting, spending on average only 0.56 per cent of turnover on R&D expenditure. Even in large firms this rises to just 0.71 per cent.[13]

The gears are grinding
You don't need an MBA from Harvard Business School to spot a potential weakness in the government's approach. China's success over the past 20 years has relied on the architecture of bureaucracy and central planning. Can the same approach be used now to encourage innovation, experimentation and change? One person who is well aware of these contradictions is Ze Zhang, the vice president of Beijing University of Technology. We met him when he had just returned from the general assembly of the Chinese Association for Science and Technology (CAST):

Everyone there was talking constantly of innovation. But I think we are only just beginning to understand what this word really means. It's like gears grinding against one another. There's a lot of tension between the push for innovation and the capacity of the political system to deliver it.[14]

A political high-flier since his youth, Professor Zhang is now approaching retirement, and is not afraid to voice a few criticisms of government policy. On the wall of his office there is a gilt-framed photograph of his class from the Party School. Proudly, he points out his colleagues: 'One became mayor of Shanghai, another is a vice-minister. These are the people who are running China.' For five years, Zhang himself played a central role in the machinery of science policy, as general secretary of CAST. He took the job in the hope of introducing reforms, but found it an uphill struggle. 'I made a few changes, but it was very hard, I tried to resign twice but my resignation was refused.'

Zhang argues that the biggest obstacles are in the private sector:

Probably the greatest challenge is to get Chinese companies to become more innovative... Reform is needed here, especially in state-owned enterprises, where the bosses are still chosen by the Party. It's not like shareholders who have the company's best interests at heart.

Another problem that has worsened in the past five years is plagiarism and research misconduct:

Again, it's the result of politics getting mixed up with science... There are policies to encourage people to generate publications and patents and prizes. You get a score and if you are an 'A', you get 25 per cent more salary. It's easy to understand why this leads people to plagiarise results. Every university has this problem. I've suffered from it myself. Some ex-students of mine took my data and published it in Science. This happened only five months ago.

Zhang worries that this upsurge in plagiarism is having a corrosive effect on research cultures within universities and institutes. 'Collaboration becomes very difficult. You can't trust people not to steal your work. Everyone works with the door closed, in secret. This is very bad for innovation.' However, he is cautiously optimistic that things may improve in response to recent science scandals:

Now misconduct has really started to attract attention. Since the Hwang case in South Korea, people are more alert to the problem, and there will be more effort to solve it. But it's not clear how easy it will be to root out.

To what extent does Zhang debate these problems with his friends and colleagues in the Party School?

In private, they talk very honestly, with lots of debate... They are good people, very open to ideas. Even so, you still have to play by the rules of the game. You have to make points in relation to Party doctrine.

So you couldn't simply recommend policies for China based on Silicon Valley or Finland?

You could, but you still have to talk about them in terms of Party language, Party theories. You can't just offer an idea from the West. They need to be Chinese ideas set in the Chinese context.

A wider debate

In 2004, the journal *Nature* published a series of articles by prominent Chinese scientists based in China and the US, intended as a contribution to early deliberations over the new 15-year plan. One recommended that the Ministry of Science and Technology (MOST) should have its powers to determine budgets removed, in favour of more peer-reviewed grants. Another lambasted waste, bureaucracy and a lack of accountability in the Chinese research system.[15] Senior officials in MOST were furious and complained to the General Administration of Press and Publication. In a manufactured row, *Nature* was also accused of publishing a map of China that excluded Taiwan. As a result, the offending *Nature* supplement was banned, and discussions of the 15-year plan in a range of Chinese publications were also censored.[16]

Since the new plan was finalised, Chinese policy-makers have become more willing to debate how it should be implemented. The readiness of scientists such as Ze Zhang to speak out perhaps reflects a more open climate. Adam Segal, a China expert at the Council on Foreign Relations, a US think tank, detects a different tone in recent interactions between Chinese and international experts on innovation:

There is a growing and refreshing scepticism among policy-makers in China about how much policy and planning can actually deliver in relation to innovation... There's no longer a simple dichotomy between top-down and bottom-up.[17]

Other commentators have observed that the scope of the plan's ambitions for independent innovation means that MOST can no longer automatically take a lead in its implementation. This allows for some re-negotiation of priorities between the different institutions that shape Chinese science policy. Prominent among these is the Chinese Academy of Sciences (CAS), which has attempted to reinvent itself in the past decade through a 'Knowledge Innovation Program', designed to secure its place as the 'backbone' of the national system of innovation. Since 1998, this package of reforms has included a dramatic reduction in the number of CAS institutes, and the recruitment of a new generation of institute directors, with the average age dropping from 56 to 47.[18] Similarly, the National Natural Science Foundation, one of China's main science funding bodies, is growing in importance. Its budget, which reached US$337 million in 2005, is set to grow by around 20 per cent each year for the next five years, and it has also pioneered the use of international peer review in the evaluation of grant proposals.

A new techno-nationalism

While there are some encouraging signs of reform and openness within the Chinese innovation system, there is also a growing undercurrent of techno-nationalism.[19] The roots of this go back to the nineteenth century and are intimately bound up with China's anxieties over falling behind the West during the industrial revolution. After the founding of the People's Republic of China (PRC) in 1949, China's reliance on Soviet technology also gave rise to calls for greater self-reliance. Today, techno-nationalism finds expression in efforts to set new technological standards, and in the desire for a Chinese scientist to win a Nobel Prize.

A central question is whether techno-nationalism will gather momentum, or whether the countervailing impulse toward global collaboration… will prove stronger.

Aspects of techno-nationalism are also reflected in a range of trophy projects. One example is China's growing ambitions in space. On 17 October 2005, after a five-day voyage, the astronauts Fei Junlong and Nie Hasheng landed safely on the remote steppes of Inner Mongolia. This was China's second successful human space flight, after an initial mission in 2003. The government described it as a technological breakthrough, and announced it was planning its first space walk for 2007. 'Let us raise a welcoming toast to our heroes,' declared the Xinhua news agency. 'At this moment, history is returning dignity and sanctity to the Chinese nation.'[20]

These sentiments are not restricted to science and technology policy. Alongside talk of a 'peaceful rise' and 'good neighbourliness', popular forms of nationalism are increasingly evident in Chinese culture and politics. Occasionally, these spill over into something more visceral, as with the anti-Japanese demonstrations of 2005, but usually they are benign. In a recent book, Christopher Hughes explores these tensions and suggests that the Chinese government has encouraged a peculiarly globalised nationalism, which has so far remained compatible with the need to attract foreign investment, technologies and knowledge.[21]

Over the next decade, as China's science and innovation capabilities grow rapidly, a central question is whether techno-nationalism will gather momentum, or whether the countervailing impulse towards global collaboration and exchange of new ideas – what we term in this report 'cosmopolitan innovation' – will prove stronger. In this context, it is interesting to reflect again on the phrase *zizhu chuangxin* that features so prominently in the 15-year plan. In an article in *People's Daily*, Professor Bai Chunli, the vice president of CAS, explains the phrase in terms of three linked aims: first, for China to produce original innovations in science and technology; second, for 'integrated innovation… a process in which many technological innovations are integrated, culminating in the production of a new product'; and third, for 're-innovation on the basis of acquiring and absorbing imported technologies'.[22]

Aspects of this definition have raised some eyebrows inside multinational companies and foreign embassies, where there are worries about the intellectual property implications of a drive to 'absorb' foreign technologies. But among Chinese scientists, too, there are unanswered questions about what this might mean. Will it lead to a reduction in support for international collaboration? And in the context of global R&D networks, how will 'independence' be defined? Might research teams eventually be penalised for involving foreign scientists or Chinese based overseas?

A gathering storm?

Speaking at a science policy forum in New York in August 2006, Shang Yong, China's vice minister for science, was keen to emphasise that *zizhu chuangxin* posed no threat to the US or other countries, but would 'boost the global economy… and bring opportunities to global industrial restructuring and upgrading as well as sustainable development, thus benefiting the whole world.'[23]

Nonetheless, there clearly are tensions here that will take some years to play out. Science and technology is one of a number of arenas in which China faces choices about how proactively to engage with international projects, networks and institutions. The main focus of this report, and the Atlas of Ideas project, is how the UK and Europe can strengthen both the political case and the practical mechanisms to underpin closer integration and collaboration with China, to the benefit of both sides.

The alternative is to turn inwards. And it is important to recognise that this is not only a danger for China, but also for Europe and the US, where the speed of economic and social change under globalisation can breed fear and suspicion of new rivals as much as it encourages collaboration. In this scenario, techno-nationalisms become mutually reinforcing: European or US over-reaction to China's perceived self-interest may fuel a more aggressive cycle of competition or protectionism. There are hints of this in the 2005 report from the US National Academies of Science, *Rising Above the Gathering Storm*, which warns that 'for the cost of one chemist or engineer in the US, a company can hire about five chemists in China or 11 engineers in India'. As a result, the US 'could soon lose its privileged position' in science, with new competitors just a 'mouse-click away'.[24]

“ ”

In the new geography of science, it is those who are good at sharing, rather than protecting knowledge, who will flourish.

In Europe, the tone may differ, but there is no disguising the existence of similar concerns. Our argument in this report is that such responses are short sighted, and ignore the opportunities that are being created by the emergence of new centres of innovation in China and elsewhere. In the new geography of science, it is those who are good at sharing, rather than protecting knowledge, who will flourish. Rather than shoring up our scientific defences, our priority should be developing better mechanisms for orchestrating research across international networks, and supporting scientists in Europe and China to collaborate in pursuit of global research goals.

It is worth reflecting on the parallels between present fears about China and those that surrounded Japan in the 1970s. Then, as now, all the talk was of a new technological superpower that threatened European and US jobs. There was an initial period of friction over currency accords and the terms of global trade. But today, how many of us sit here lamenting Japan's contributions to global innovation as we tap away on our Sony laptops? Just as we have benefited from Japan's rise, so we can benefit from advances in China. This is not to underplay elements of competitive challenge, which clearly exist. But as much as it is a competitor, China is also a trading partner, a potential research collaborator, and a huge market for European goods and services.

We start in the next chapter by mapping some of the main developments and key actors in Chinese science and innovation, and asking whether the headline numbers give an accurate sense of where things are heading. Politicians in Europe and the US constantly draw attention to the sheer volume of scientists and engineers that are pouring out of China's universities. In chapter 3, we look behind these statistics to understand more about the strengths and weaknesses of the R&D workforce, and we consider the role that returnees from abroad will play in developing China's capacity for innovation.

Chapter 4 describes how the geographical distribution of R&D in China is changing, and highlights some of the cities and provinces that are likely to grow in significance over the next decade. This is partly a story about new flows of business R&D, and in chapter 5 we look at the role that corporate innovation will play, as practised by multinationals and domestic companies.

Chapter 6 explores less tangible aspects of the innovation system: the ethics, values and research cultures that will be as important as money, people and places if China is to succeed. We outline some recent problems in this area, but reject simplistic notions of Chinese science as a 'wild east' unencumbered by ethical concerns.

In chapter 7, our focus returns to the UK and Europe. We describe current approaches to collaboration with China and suggest how these might be improved. And in chapter 8, we tackle the question posed in the title of this report, by reviewing the strengths and weaknesses in the Chinese system, the balance of which will determine whether it does eventually become a scientific 'superpower'. We argue against a retreat into techno-nationalism, and call instead for a model of cosmopolitan innovation in pursuit of global public goods – for example in relation to climate change, poverty alleviation and the treatment of neglected diseases. Finally, we end with a series of recommendations on how this positive agenda for collaboration can be taken forward.

Knowledge is power

This report provides only a snapshot of science and innovation in China. It is impossible to do justice to the diversity of a country of 1.3 billion people spread over 3.7 million square miles. In a recent essay, Joshua Cooper Ramo speaks of the difficulty of finding a national framework

capable of containing both the lively energy of Shanghai and the grinding poverty of Gansu, both the joy of expanding liberty and the too-frequent chill of restricted freedom, both the warm hearts of the Chinese people and their deep fear of social instability and foreign influence.[25]

Our ambition here is more modest: to provide an overview of the factors that will shape Chinese science and innovation over the next decade; to assess the likely balance of opportunities and constraints; and to suggest how the UK, Europe and China can scale up their levels of research collaboration.

Generalisation is one pitfall. Another is to overstate the novelty of what is happening. It is a cliché of reports on Chinese science to rehearse the long list of innovations that China introduced to the world in pre-modern times: from gunpowder and printing to porcelain and windmills. Why this inventiveness stalled has long been the subject of debate among historians of science.[26] But connecting current developments to their historical and cultural antecedents can serve a wider purpose.

It reminds us that China is not necessarily in a 'race' to the same destination as Europe or the US. If we view the world only in terms of GERD ratios,[27] graduate numbers and patent filings – the nuts and bolts of a typical innovation systems analysis – we lose sight of a more fundamental but open-ended set of questions.

Science is caught up in a bigger, unfolding debate about the pace, scale and direction of China's economic and political reforms. Given the levels of investment and ambition represented by the new 15-year plan, there can be little doubt that China will be a growing force in global science and innovation over the next decade and beyond. But a lot still depends on the playing out of a complicated set of tensions: between the planned economy and the market; national and global priorities; the hardware of research infrastructure and the software of culture and ethics; and the skills and creativity of the scientific workforce and the entrepreneurialism and networks of returnees.

In charting possible futures for Chinese science, we must resist the temptation to ask only 'how much? or 'how fast?', and instead start to consider 'which direction?', 'says who?' and 'why?'[28] Following a decade of chaos and destruction during the Cultural Revolution, China's innovation system had to be rebuilt from scratch. To have come so far, so fast in just 30 years is little short of astonishing. Looking ahead, as China begins to tackle a fresh set of daunting social and environmental challenges, the big unknown is whether it might choose to direct its growing capabilities for innovation towards an alternative vision of development, more sustainable than our own. In the decades to come, China is likely to change science just as much as science changes China.

A note on methodology

The research for this report was carried out over 18 months by Demos, with the support of an expert steering group. The UK part of the project included a series of research seminars, two of which focused on China.

Three months were spent doing fieldwork in China. Cities visited include Beijing, Shanghai, Guangzhou, Shenzhen, Chongqing, Chengdu and Kunming. In-depth interviews and a handful of focus groups were conducted with around 170 people from government, foreign embassies, business, academia and the media. The project team also participated in conferences on Chinese science and innovation in Beijing, London and New York. A list of organisations interviewed is provided at the end of the pamphlet.

2 Mapping
Painting by numbers

'Science can be like the Olympics. Twenty years ago, at the Los Angeles Olympics, China got very few medals. But in Athens, we got 32 golds, compared to 35 for the US. Who knows what we will achieve in 2008 in Beijing? And what is true on the sports field is also true in the laboratory.'

Professor Zihe Rao, Director, CAS Institute of Biophysics

Among the 150 million items stored at the British Library in London are many of the treasures of European thought: the Magna Carta, one of Leonardo da Vinci's notebooks, Einstein's calculations and the handwritten lyrics to The Beatles' 'All You Need Is Love'. A copy of every book and article published in the UK must by law be deposited there, enabling the Library to serve as the custodian of the nation's scientific and cultural heritage.

In April 2006, a flurry of headlines greeted the Library's decision to alter its acquisition strategy. From this year, it intends to give greater priority to material from China and India. 'We want the balance of our collection to reflect changes in the global knowledge base,' explains Ann Clarke, the library's head of planning. 'There is such enormous growth in the number of publications from China, and we feel that UK researchers will benefit from better access to this material.'[29]

Following the paper trail
Bibliometrics, the analysis of publications and citations, is one way of measuring a nation's scientific output, with a variety of methods that can be deployed. For China, these reveal some interesting, if complicated, trends. In terms of the *quantity* of scientific publications, China's contribution has risen sharply, from around 2 per cent of the world share in 1995 to 6.5 per cent in 2004 (see table 2). At the present rate of growth, it will overtake the UK on this indicator within the next two years.

Table 2 Percentage of world share of scientific publications

	China	France	Germany	Japan	Korea	UK	US	EU-15
1995	2.05	6.09	7.62	8.65	0.79	8.88	33.54	34.36
1998	2.90	6.48	8.82	9.42	1.41	9.08	31.63	36.85
2001	4.30	6.33	8.68	9.52	2.01	8.90	31.01	36.55
2004	6.52	5.84	8.14	8.84	2.70	8.33	30.48	35.18

Source: Adapted from P Zhou and L Leydesdorff, 'The emergence of China as a leading nation in science', *Research Policy* 35, no 1 (Feb 2006).

One person who is well placed to monitor these trends is Paul Evans, vice president of Elsevier in China. When we met Paul in his Beijing office, he was open about how crucial China is to the future of the business:

Elsevier publishes around 1800 academic journals. Within three to four years, we expect China to overtake the US in terms of the quantity of papers being published. This is a huge market for us.[30]

There are several reasons for this growth. PhD students are now expected to publish at least one article in a journal listed in Thomson's *Science Citation Index*, the main citation database. For more experienced academics, publication records are increasingly used to determine funding.

Researchers can also win prizes and awards for publishing in highly ranked journals. One told us: 'If you were to get a paper in *Nature* or *Science*, you would get a 50,000 RMB bonus from the university and also extra research funds from the government.'[31] But as Paul Evans describes, this remorseless drive to publish does have its downsides:

The pressure on PhD students has led to a flood of poor quality papers, which can distract attention from the top quality work that's being done. It's a headache for our journal editors... and I think it's been bad for the overall reputation of Chinese science. Typically we reject around 50 per cent of the papers we receive from the US, and around 80 per cent from China.

The *quality* of publications is normally measured through citations. Here, as Paul Evans indicates, China's record is more mixed. From 1993 to 2003, there were no Chinese in the top 20 most cited international scientists and only two in the top 100.[32] In a well-known *Nature* article, Sir David King, the UK's chief scientist, ranked China in nineteenth position, according to its share of the most highly cited publications between 1993 and 2001.[33] Yet some have criticised King's approach for aggregating diverse subject fields into a single number – 'comparing apples with oranges'[34] – and for underestimating the more significant contribution of China to emerging fields such as nanotechnology.[35]

In their own assessment, bibliometric experts Loet Leydesdorff and Ping Zhou acknowledge that China's citation rate is low, but attribute this more to language and cultural factors than to poor-quality science. They note that until 2004, only 78 Chinese language journals (out of a total of 4420) were included in the *Science Citation Index*. They also point out that the ability of a researcher to achieve high citation rates depends not only on the originality of their work, but also on their communication skills and visibility within global networks – qualities which are perhaps harder to find among Chinese scientists than their European or US counterparts.

At the level of specific disciplines, the picture is yet more complicated, and it seems fair to argue that the aggregate figures used by King may obscure areas of strength. In some fields, such as material science, analytical chemistry and rice genomics, there is no doubt that China's performance is particularly strong. For example, a recent analysis of nanoscience publications shows that China now ranks third globally, just behind Japan, with the US some way ahead (see figure 1).

Figure 1 Number of scientific publications in nanoscience by country, 1999–2004

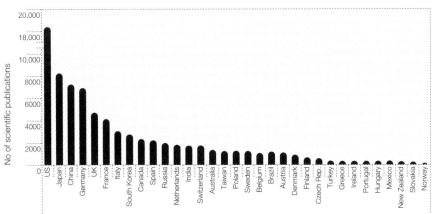

Source: From A Hullman, 'Who is winning the global nanorace?', *Nature Nanotechnology* 1, no 81–83 (2006).

Similarly, national figures conceal strong performances by some individual universities. One study found that Beijing University was among the top 1 per cent of world institutions in citations for physics, chemistry, engineering, materials, mathematics and clinical medicine. Five other Chinese universities were in the top 1 per cent for at least one of these fields.[36] Table 3 shows which institutions are most prolific in terms of publishing output.

Table 3 Most prolific Chinese institutions in terms of publications, 2004/05

Institution		Number of papers
1	Chinese Academy of Sciences	7029
2	Tsinghua University	1886
3	Zhejiang University	1477
4	Beijing University	1391
5	Shanghai Jiao Tong University	1204
6	University of Hong Kong	1098
7	University of Science and Technology, China	943
8	Nanjing University	940
9	Fudan University	905
10	Chinese University of Hong Kong	880

Source: R Kostoff et al, *The Structure and Infrastructure of Chinese Science and Technology* (Fort Belvoir, VA: Defense Technical Information Center, 2006).

In an effort to compensate for the dominance of English language publications, China has now established two citation indices of its own, but neither of these has yet received global recognition.[37] At the same time, foreign publishers are taking a closer interest in Chinese language journals. In March 2006, Elsevier announced that it would publish 34 Chinese journals in English through its online database ScienceDirect. Paul Evans explains:

We're trying to pick up some of the higher quality journals before anyone else does. There's a bit of a goldrush on at the moment. It can be a lot of work translating them, and none of them are yet taking international papers from non-Chinese authors. But ultimately a national model isn't enough: to be world-class, these journals need to take international papers. That's why we're running training for Chinese journal editors, basically trying to build up that global capacity.

Another potential means of boosting Chinese citations that is being considered in policy circles is to promote open access publishing, which allow papers to be viewed without charge. There is some evidence that papers published in this way are cited more frequently, particularly in the developing world, where journal subscriptions may be prohibitive.[38] Paul Evans is predictably wary of open access, but acknowledges that it has some high-profile supporters, including the chief librarian at CAS. However, he remains confident that the existing model will survive: 'So far, China shows no appetite to take on the publishers and try and reinvent the scientific publishing industry.'

The headline statistics
Publication and citation data is helpful, but it by no means give a complete picture of the health or otherwise of a country's innovation system. Table 4 captures some other important numbers.

Table 4 Headline statistics

	Quantity	Year	Source
GDP growth rate	9.9%	2005	National Bureau of Statistics, China/MOST
% GDP spent on R&D	1.3%	2005	
GDP total	18,232 billion RMB	2005	
Government R&D budget	71.6 billion RMB	2005	
Annual rate of growth in government R&D budget	19.2%	2005	
S&T workforce	2.25 million scientists and engineers	2004	National Bureau of Statistics, China
	1.15 million person years spent on R&D	2004	
Enrolment in tertiary education	15 million	2004	Ministry of Education
Enrolment in postgraduate programmes	820,000	2004	
Number of science, medicine and engineering undergraduates	6,508,541	2004	
Number of science, medicine and engineering postgraduates	502,303	2004	
PhDs awarded	23,500 (70% in science-related subjects)	2004	
Number of students studying abroad (1978–2003)	700,000	1978–2003	
Number of overseas students returned to China (by 2003)	170,000	2003	
Number of colleges and universities	1731	2004	Ministry of Education
Number of graduate schools/research institutes	769	2004	Ministry of Education
Number of universities in global top 200	6 (Beijing, 14; Tsinghua, 28; Fudan, 116; China University of Science and Technology, 165; Shanghai Jiao Tong, 179; Nanjing, 180)	2006	Times Higher Education Supplement

	Quantity	Year	Source
Number of universities in global top 100 for science	5 (Beijing, 12; China University of Science and Technology, 32; Tsinghua, 41; Fudan, 63; Nanjing, 70)	2006	*Times Higher Education Supplement*
ICT uptake	390 million mobile phone users	2005	*The Economist*
	111 million internet users	2005	
Number of scientific publications (in SCI)	13,500 46,000	1995 2004	Evidence Ltd
Share of world citations	0.92% 3.78%	1995 2004	
Applications for invention patents	130,000 (around half from multinationals)	2005	State Intellectual Property Office of China (SIPO)
Growth rate of invention patent applications	23% annually since 2000	2005	SIPO
Share of total applications for invention patents	Foreign companies: 86% Chinese companies: 18%	2005	SIPO
Chinese enterprises that have never applied for patents	99%	2005	SIPO
National share of international patents filed with World Intellectual Property Organization	1.4%	2005	WIPO
US patents granted to Chinese applicants	424	2003	US Patent and Trademark Office
Inflows of foreign direct investment	US$72.6 billion	2005	United Nations Conference on Trade and Development *World Investment Report*
Multinational R&D centres in China	750	2005	Chinese Ministry of Commerce
Multinational centres performing innovative R&D	c. 60	2006	Swedish Institute for Growth Policy Studies
Chinese companies in top 500 global companies by R&D investment	4 (PetroChina, 185; China Petroleum, 260; ZTE, 298; Lenovo, 356)	2006	UK DTI global scoreboard

	Quantity	Year	Source
Value of Chinese high-tech exports	US$165.5 billion	2004	*China Yearbook on High Technology Industry*
Forbes magazine top 1000 billionaires	8 Chinese	2006	*Forbes* magazine
Gross income per capita	US$1290	2004	UNICEF
% of population living below US$1 a day	17	2003	
Average life expectancy at birth	72 years	2004	
Total adult literacy rate	91%	2004	
Deloitte Competitiveness Index	24 (out of 25 countries)	2005	Deloitte
World Economic Forum Global Competitiveness Index	54 (out of 125 countries)	2006	WEF
World Economic Forum Network Readiness Index	41 (out of 104 countries)	2006	WEF/INSEAD
Transparency International Corruption Perceptions Index	70 (out of 163 countries)	2006	Transparency International

Gathering accurate data in a country the size of China is never easy. Writing in the *Financial Times*, Guy de Jonquieres likens the challenge confronting China's economic managers to 'piloting a speeding jumbo jet half-blindfolded, relying on wildly inaccurate instruments and controls that respond sluggishly, if at all'.[39] Entire chapters could be written on the subtleties and potential interpretations of each of the statistics in table 4. But the dominant message to emerge is just how fast the innovation system is changing. As recently as 2001, the World Bank could publish a report *China and the Knowledge Economy* in which it concluded: 'The number of Chinese scientific articles... remains low at 1.4 per cent... More generally, it is hard to find science and technology fields in which China is a world leader.'[40] Five years on, such assessments are already outdated, and the big question is how different things may look again in five, ten or 15 years from now.

It can be difficult for perceptions and attitudes outside China to keep pace with the speed of developments. Linear projections based on conventional indicators are a poor guide to what will happen next. The situation is further complicated by the way that national innovation systems are now intimately bound up in global networks and flows of knowledge, capital and talent. At a Tsinghua University conference on innovation in May 2006, Richard P Suttmeier admitted that this poses as much of a challenge for the experts as for everyone else:

It's no longer possible to do a classic national innovation systems analysis, to tick all the boxes. The sheer complexity of these relationships, the unintended consequences, the feedback loops are intensely difficult to analyse... The nature of global innovation is changing, and we need to update our frameworks and models to take account of this.[41]

The policy players

In a recent book on China's rise, James Kynge describes a common misperception that outsiders have about the way change has occurred:

In the popular imagination, the launch of China's economic reforms in 1978 was a planned, top-down affair managed by a man who is often called the 'architect' of the country's emergence, Deng Xiaoping.

By this account, Beijing has all along been implementing a master plan that has delivered structured, gradual reforms. But, says Kynge, 'the reality has not been so neat. Many of the key events and occurrences that propelled progress towards capitalism were, in fact, either unplanned, unintended or completely accidental.'[42] The same is likely to apply to the next phase of developments in Chinese science. The 15-year plan provides a helpful sense of what central government would like to see happen, but many of the determining factors now lie beyond its direct control. Science and innovation can be found in many places: universities, research institutes, multinational R&D centres and Chinese companies, both large and small. That said, it is still important to know who the principal actors in the policy arena are, and how their agendas align or collide. Figure 2 details who's who.

Figure 2 Key institutions in Chinese science and innovation policy

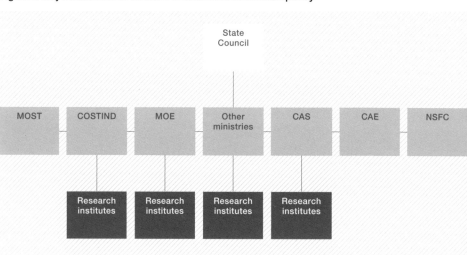

The State Council is the highest administrative body in China. Beneath it, there are six ministry-level organisations that deal with science and innovation.

— *Ministry of Science and Technology (MOST)*
Created in 1998 out of the former State Science and Technology Commission, MOST has the primary responsibility for science and technology policy and strategy. It finances a large amount of research, primarily through special programmes such as 863, 973 and Torch.[43] It also administers technological development zones and oversees international collaboration.

— *Commission of Science, Technology and Industry for National Defence (COSTIND)*
Formed in 1982, this influential but secretive body oversees defence-related R&D and military applications of commercial technologies.

— *Ministry of Education (MOE)*
The MOE is responsible for education policy and management of higher education institutions. It also oversees state key laboratories and research institutes in universities, and has established various initiatives to promote the commercialisation of scientific research.

— *Chinese Academy of Sciences (CAS)*
Formed in 1949, CAS is China's most prestigious science organisation, and its academicians (*yuanshi*) are the scientific elite. Following recent reforms under its 'Knowledge Innovation Programme', CAS now runs 89 research institutes which have spun out several hundred companies. It also runs research programmes, graduate training schemes, and has an important role in providing policy advice and scientific input to government.[44]

— *Chinese Academy of Engineering (CAE)*
Created more recently, in 1994, CAE has around 600 academicians and is involved in policy advice and development. Unlike CAS, it does not run its own research institutes.

— *National Natural Science Foundation of China (NSFC)*
The NSFC was set up in 1986 to promote and support scientific research. Its budget in 2005 was US$337 million, which is around one-fifth of the government's total investment in research. In May 2006, it was announced that the NSFC's budget will increase by around 20 per cent a year until 2010.[45]

Mapping the frontiers
There are different ways of trying to gauge how Chinese science and innovation is changing. One is to look at the latest data on inputs and outputs. Another is to chart the evolving responsibilities and interactions between key institutions. A third is to focus on a few high-profile and emblematic areas of frontier science and assess how China is performing here.

Two areas that are attracting large amounts of attention and investment in China, as they are elsewhere, are nanotechnology and stem cell biology. These fields are important in terms of their medical and technological potential, but also because the expectations of policy-makers and investors have created 'economies of promise' that will intensify the pressure on scientists to deliver quick results.[46] How does China's progress in these fields compare with developments elsewhere?

— *Nanoscience and nanotechnologies*
Over the next 20 years, nanoscience is expected to produce radical innovations in IT, pharmaceuticals, nerve and tissue repair, surface coatings, catalysts, sensors and pollution control. Global research funding is increasing rapidly, and is estimated to have reached US$8.6 billion in 2004.[47] China ranks ninth in the world, with US$111 million of funding in 2004 (around one-tenth of what the US spends). This is already yielding impressive results: as noted earlier, China is now third after the US and Japan in the quantity of nanoscience publications it produces (and second in the subfield of nanomaterials).[48] The Chinese Academy of Sciences is ranked fourth in the world for nano citations after UC Berkeley, MIT and IBM.[49] According to the China Association for Science and Technology, the three most widely used high-tech words in China today are 'computer', 'gene' and 'nanometer'.

4th

The Chinese Academy of Sciences is ranked fourth in the world for nano citations after UC Berkeley, MIT and IBM.

Chunli Bai is one of China's most celebrated nanoscientists, and an early pioneer of scanning tunnelling microscopy. As vice president of CAS, he has also been an influential voice in furthering China's advances in this field. Writing in *Science*, he concludes that:

The nanoscience and nanotechnology community in China has made remarkable advances across the R&D spectrum, from fundamental scientific research to studies into the potential societal implications of new nanotechnologies.[50]

His colleague Chen Wang, who is deputy director of the National Centre for Nanoscience and Technology in Beijing, agrees:

In terms of citations, our strengths are still underestimated by what is in the academic literature. People like to reference the people they already know, and our nanoscientists aren't yet well known. But this will change.[51]

— *Stem cell biology*
The potential of stem cell research to produce therapies for diseases such as Alzheimer's and Parkinson's, and novel techniques for tissue repair and regenerative medicine, has prompted a flood of research and investment worldwide. China has been active in stem cell research since it emerged in the late 1990s, and now has at least 300 researchers working in the field, spread over 30 institutions. Adult stem cell research is the main focus, although there are at least ten embryonic stem cell lines also in use across the country.[52] Between 2006 and 2010, MOST expects to spend between 500 million RMB and 2 billion RMB in this area, depending on the amount of progress being made. Notable achievements so far include:

— the first clinical trials of adult stem cells as a treatment for traumatic brain injuries, led by neurosurgeon Jianhong Zhu at Fudan University; his patients, who have mostly suffered 'chopstick injury' as the result of arguments over a meal, are treated with neural stem cells extracted from their wounds, cultured and then reinserted
— the successful cloning of several animal species, including goats, pigs, cattle, mice and the first successful cloning of a rat
— the first use of cultured stem cell lines from human fetuses in large-scale transplantation studies in primates
— the establishment of a network of cord blood stem cell banks across China, for research and clinical use.[53]

One distinctive feature of Chinese stem cell research is the enthusiasm there is for applying the findings in a clinical context. Stephen Minger, director of the Stem Cell Biology Laboratory at the Wolfson Centre, King's College London, says that China could derive a distinct advantage from the speed of its clinical translation:

It's a different cultural climate. If you discover something that you think is of clinical benefit, it's seen as unethical if you don't use it as soon as possible to treat patients. You still need to do the appropriate safety and toxicity trials but the overall transition from basic to clinical research is a lot faster.[54]

Professor Minger was part of a UK delegation in 2004 which travelled to China, Korea and Singapore to assess their capabilities in stem cell research. He describes how the trip challenged his preconceptions:

They had just built six or seven brand new laboratories, all of them kitted out with better equipment than I have here in London.
Professor Stephen Minger

I went over there with this idea that China would be behind – that there would be very basic infrastructure. We arrived in Beijing and went out the next day to a heavily guarded research institute. It was old and dusty, and had an air of faded grandeur. We were met by a French woman scientist. The first lab she took us to was ghastly, awful – everything looked 100 years old. It reinforced all my worst expectations. And, I thought, why on earth is she working here? Why would anybody leave Paris to come and work in this environment? Then she said, 'Let me take you across to the cloning labs.' So we walked down the corridor and came to a glass laboratory that had been built as a completely new structure inside the shell of the old building. It was state of the art – as good as anything I've seen in the UK or US. They had just built six or seven brand new laboratories, all of them kitted out with better equipment than I have here in London.[55]

Adding it all up

Whether in relation to publications and citations or levels of investment in cutting-edge science, the aggregate numbers now coming out of China are impressive. But they still tell us only part of the story. There is no straightforward path from quantity to quality. Alongside excellence, there is unevenness: in certain areas of science, done in particular places, China is world class, even while the rest of the system lags behind. Raising overall performance across the innovation system will require sustained efforts to link the hardware of investment and infrastructure to the software of culture, values and creativity. Statistics will always struggle to convey the diversity and abundance of China's human resources, and it is to the contribution of people that we now turn.

3 People
Sea-turtle soup

Top five destination countries for tertiary level
Chinese students studying abroad in 2004
(total 343,126)

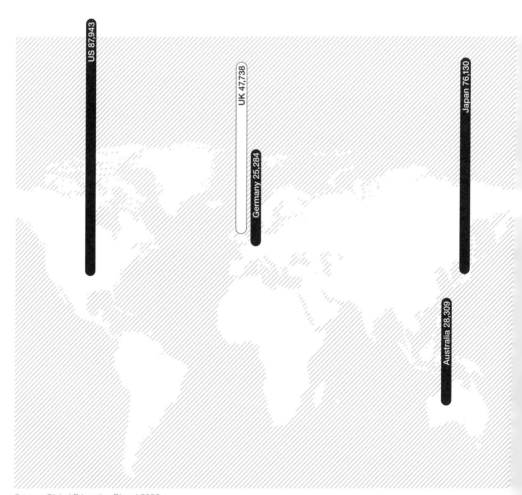

US 87,943

UK 47,738

Germany 25,284

Japan 76,130

Australia 28,309

Source: *Global Education Digest 2006*

Li Gong had more or less given up on the idea of returning to China. After 13 years away, he was comfortably established in Silicon Valley as a top software architect for Sun Microsystems. But in 2000, he received an offer that was difficult to refuse: 'The CEO of Sun said to me, you're our most senior Chinese engineer. We want to start doing R&D in China and we want you to go back and run it.' He thought hard before accepting:

But the internet was booming. Multinationals were starting to open R&D labs. A lot of my friends were encouraging me to come back. And Sun wanted me to set up their operations from scratch, which I knew would be a huge challenge. My wife was less sure, but we talked it through, and eventually decided to return to Beijing.[56]

Li Gong's journey, from east to west and back again, is typical of a generation of Chinese scientists and engineers. Born in 1963, he left school in 1980 and managed, despite fierce competition, to get a place to study computer science at Tsinghua University:

At my school, if you asked a group of kids what they wanted to be, 95 per cent of them would say a scientist. There were all sorts of slogans about saving the nation through science, so the brightest and best were naturally attracted to science and engineering.

Even at a prestigious university like Tsinghua, computer science was at this stage way behind Europe and US:

Mine was a five-year course, but it wasn't until 1983 that I got to touch my first IBM computer... We had to wear special clothes and cover our hair before we were even allowed to handle them.

After graduation, many of Gong's friends went to the US. He considered doing the same, but then heard about an opportunity to go to the UK on a Sino–British Friendship Scholarship Scheme that had been established in the run-up to the handover of Hong Kong through a donation from the shipping magnate YK Pao. Gong applied and won a place to study a PhD at Cambridge under the eminent computer scientists Roger Needham and David Wheeler. The style of teaching was very different from Tsinghua:

My supervisor was extremely hands off. He never told me what to do. His approach was to drop you in the middle of a pond and let you swim and find your own way out. But I liked that a lot and in the end I completed my PhD quickly, in around two and a half years.

In 1989, Gong began making plans to return home, and wrote to Tsinghua to see if they would offer him a research position. But events that June in Tiananmen Square changed his mind:

At the time, I was president of the Chinese Students Association in Cambridge, and suddenly I realised that after three years of being able to speak my mind freely, if I returned I would have to keep my mouth shut. So this wasn't a very attractive option. A lot of people who were supposed to go back at that time didn't.

He looked for research or teaching posts in the UK, but jobs in the emerging field of computer security, the focus of his PhD research, were hard to come by. So he turned instead to the US, and eventually found a job with a computer security start-up in New York.

In 1993, he abandoned the east coast and moved to Silicon Valley. He started working at Stanford Research Institute (SRI), and quickly developed a name for himself in computer security. Then the internet began to take off. He started talking to the designers of Java, a new programming language and software platform that Sun Microsystems was developing:

52,000

Even within the melting pot of Silicon Valley, the Chinese were the largest group, with around 52,000 highly skilled workers moving to the area between 1985 and 2000.

Java had a big security problem, and they asked me to help them fix it. So I joined JavaSoft as the Chief Java Security Architect... It was an amazing period to be working in Silicon Valley.

Gong was still working on Java applications when Sun invited him to return to China. From the start, he was adamant that he wanted to do world-class research. 'I said, let me show you. If you give me a team that's just half the size of the browser team in the US, I can do it here.' The lab grew quickly, reaching 400 people at its peak. Many of the staff were young graduates from Chinese universities, and one of Gong's main challenges was to encourage them to be creative:

I told people, leave your assumptions at the door. So people started wearing sandals to work. It caused a bit of a stir. We introduced a tea-time at 3.30 on Friday afternoons, for people to talk and share ideas. The first time we did it, everyone gathered expectantly as if they wanted me to give a speech. And I said no, this is a time for you to talk to one another!

In 2005, Gong decided to move on from Sun. 'The company was declining financially. It wasn't as innovative as it had been.' It is a tribute to his management style that 150 of his colleagues quit with him. After considering a number of jobs in academia and business, he accepted an offer from Microsoft to run Windows Live in China.

Five years after returning to China, Gong has no regrets about his decision. But he does occasionally feel frustrated that returnees are kept at the margins of Chinese national life. He explains: 'There is some resentment towards returnees. People are happy that we have come back to make money and share our knowledge, but we are kept outside the centre, in the import zone.' With a group of friends and colleagues, Gong is now doing his bit to address this problem:

Last year, it was the twentieth anniversary of my graduating class at Tsinghua, and they asked me to give a speech. I ended up saying, 'Look, we all left in '85. When we left we were at the centre of China, we were in the mainstream of the mainstream. But now 20 years later, after so many of us have been abroad, who is in the mainstream? We need to start a movement of those who want to return to the mainstream.' This idea created a real buzz. So we started a 'mainstream forum', mostly for people from my year at Tsinghua, but also a few others. It's a place for people to share their experiences. It's for those who want to influence government and the institutions that exercise power in Chinese society.

The new Argonauts
Different versions of Li Gong's story could be told by many of the Chinese diaspora who have now returned. In 1978, after the lost decade of the Cultural Revolution, Chinese graduates again started to travel abroad for further study. Over the next 25 years, 700,000 followed suit. The vast majority stayed on in the US or Europe to work and are still resident overseas. But in the past five or six years, what was a trickle of returnees has become a steady flow. On some estimates, 170,000 people have been attracted back by a mix of national loyalty, family ties, government incentives and the entrepreneurial opportunities offered by a booming economy.[57]

The economic geographer AnnaLee Saxenian has traced the movements of these skilled diasporas and their contribution to high-tech regions such as Silicon Valley. In a recent book, she describes them as 'the new Argonauts', who 'like the Greeks who sailed with Jason... undertake the risky but economically rewarding project of starting companies far from established centres of skill and technology'.[58] The conventional assumption is that new technologies will emerge in highly developed nations, with more peripheral regions destined to follow rather than lead. This model, argues Saxenian, is now breaking down: 'The new Argonauts are undermining the old pattern of one-way flows of technology and capital from the core to the periphery, creating far more complex and decentralised two-way flows of skills, capital and technology.'[59]

Policy-makers in developing countries used to be concerned about a 'brain drain', as their most talented students headed overseas. Few people saw that these migrant scientists, engineers and entrepreneurs might one day become an asset. But notions of brain drain have now been superseded by a recognition of the value of 'brain circulation', as thousands of these people return home to start new companies or take up senior posts in academia, while maintaining useful links back to the US or Europe.

Like Li Gong, many of those who studied abroad ended up working in Silicon Valley. The openness of its working cultures, the respect given to technical expertise, and the speed with which ideas could be capitalised and turned into businesses, made Silicon Valley the ideal environment for entrepreneurial migrants. Many rose quickly to prominent positions. Saxenian records a joke doing the rounds in the late 1990s: 'When we say that Silicon Valley is built on ICs, we don't mean integrated circuits – we mean Indians and Chinese.'[60] Even within the melting pot of Silicon Valley, the Chinese were the largest group, with around 52,000 highly skilled workers moving to the area between 1985 and 2000 (see figure 3). As they grew, these communities formed their own associations and networks, to support the transfer of experience and help newcomers to settle in.

Figure 3 Professional and technical immigrants to the San Francisco Bay Area, 1985–2000

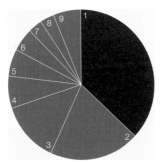

1	China
2	India
3	Taiwan
4	Iran
5	Russia
6	Korea
7	Vietnam
8	Mexico
9	Other

Source: A Saxenian, *The New Argonauts: Regional advantage in a global economy.*

Homeward bound

In her history of the Chinese diaspora, *Sons of the Yellow Emperor*, Lynn Pan locates this latest wave of migrants within a long tradition.[61] There have, she argues, been four main varieties of Chinese working overseas. The earliest were the traders, artisans and skilled workers who established trading networks elsewhere in south-east Asia in the eighteenth and nineteenth centuries. These were followed by peasants and contract labourers who travelled to the US and Australia in the late nineteenth century to work in the rapidly expanding mines and plantations.

The third type was the 'hua-ch'iao', patriotic Chinese who travelled abroad in the first half of the twentieth century, often working as diplomats. Today, the largest category is educated professionals, mostly western-educated, who have settled in Europe, Australia and the US.

Deborah Seligsohn, science counsellor at the US Embassy in Beijing, describes the flow of skilled Chinese back in the past three or four years as 'a very visible trend'.[62] The dot-com crash of 2001 and the high-tech recession that followed was one reason why growing numbers decided to return. For those wanting to work in academic research, there were also attractive incentives on offer from the Chinese government, through schemes such as the '100 Talents' programme, which offers high salaries and generous research budgets to promising scientists under the age of 45. Between 1998 and 2004, 899 researchers were recruited in this way.[63] Jiang Zhu, deputy director of CAS Institute of Atmospheric Physics, did a PhD at Lancaster University in the UK, but was lured back as one of the '100 talents'. He explained to us how the scheme works:

I got a call from China and they offered me 2 million RMB over three years for a research grant. They said that 20 per cent of this could be put towards the costs of an apartment. So I thought this was a very attractive offer. I applied, was interviewed and got offered the job.[64]

A similar programme was launched in 2005 by the NSFC, offering annual grants of up to 1 million RMB (US$120,000) for four years to overseas Chinese scientists willing to return.

17/18

At one institute we visited... 17 of the 18 principal investigators are returnees from the US or Canada.

There are many different types of returnees: entrepreneurs, multinational managers, academic researchers and investors. Their motivations for returning vary. We had dinner with a group of returnee scientists and entrepreneurs in Shanghai. One explained: 'It's a mix of national pride, culture and career advancement. Yes, people are happy to contribute to China's development. But primarily we want to do well in business or in science.'[65] As the numbers of returnees grow, they are able to transfer aspects of the Silicon Valley entrepreneurial system to the new knowledge centres of Shanghai, Beijing, Guangzhou and Shenzhen. When their ideas, management skills, contacts and access to venture capital are added to what is already there, new business opportunities quickly emerge.

The benefits are also visible in an academic setting. At one institute we visited, the CAS Institute for Biomedicine and Health in Guangzhou, 17 of the 18 principal investigators are returnees from the US or Canada. There are gains on both sides from this process of brain circulation. One of the directors, Biliang Zhang, explained:

Having us back in China running an institute is actually very useful for our colleagues in the US. It means we have a bridge on which to build collaboration. I'm now setting up a joint venture with my former professor in Massachusetts, which will be headquartered in the US, but take advantage of the cheaper research costs here.[66]

Hai gui or hai dai?
Those who come back to China are commonly nicknamed 'sea-turtles', from the term 'hai gui', which in Mandarin means returnee but also sounds like sea-turtle. And when someone who has come back from overseas fails to secure a job, he or she becomes a 'job-waiting returnee', or 'hai dai' for short. As a homonym of 'seaweed', this term has given rise to a host of returnee-related jokes, which reflect a certain ambivalence towards them as a group.

Li Gong is not alone in sometimes feeling frustrated at being kept at arm's length. Many of the returnees we interviewed expressed similar views. Jin Kewen, who was part of an early wave of returnees to Shanghai in the 1990s, argues that it depends what you come back to do:

If you work in research, or for a multinational, then generally you do better as a returnee. If you work for a Chinese company, especially one that's consumer-based, it's a handicap to have returned. In some sectors, those who stay have got far better knowledge and networks than we have.[67]

After five years of steady increases in their numbers, there are the beginnings of a backlash from those who feel that returnees are being overpaid or unfairly promoted ahead of local talent. Within the science community, particular resentment has been directed towards the *jiangzuo*, overseas academics who take highly paid associate positions in Chinese institutions, but are required to work in China for only two or three months of the year. In July 2005, Shing-Tung Yau, a Harvard mathematician, caused a storm when he dismissed most of the foreign recruits to Beijing University as 'fakes', during an interview with a Chinese magazine.[68] Yet this has not prevented an expansion of the *jiangzuo* programme, as Chinese universities seek to share in the credit that these international scholars gain from their work elsewhere. The number of publications with Chinese authors listing multiple affiliations is rising. 'Some high profile papers appear to come from China, even though the science didn't take root [there],' complains Mu-Ming Poo, himself a *jiangzuo* with posts at Berkeley and the Institute of Neuroscience in Shanghai.[69]

It is not clear whether the emphasis on independent innovation in the 15-year plan will lead to a further hardening of attitudes towards returnees. The strongest argument against this is that China still needs to attract back more of its scientists and engineers. The 20 per cent who have come back are already having a major impact, but it is widely assumed that the 80 per cent who remain overseas include many of the best and brightest. More flexible models, such as the *jiangzuo* programme, may be the only way of tempting these people back, even if for just one or two months of the year.

For those who have returned, another question is whether they plan to stay in China for good. The returnees we spoke to were reluctant to commit to this. Some still educate their children in the US or Europe. Others are keen to maintain their foreign citizenship, because of the long-term unpredictability of Chinese politics. Jin Kewen sums up the attitude of many:

If the US is playing sport, we cheer the US. If China is playing, we cheer China. And if the US is playing China, we cheer China. But no-one gets rid of their green card or their US passport. We may have come home but we will always keep our options open.[70]

China's creative class

The sea-turtles are an important group within China's growing 'creative class'. But we must be careful not to overplay their significance. As well as attracting people back in unprecedented numbers, China is producing more high-quality professionals of its own than ever before. One key factor is the expansion of Chinese universities. There are now 4.2 million new students per year, four times the figure in the mid-1990s, and a large percentage of these are studying science, engineering and IT.

Universities are also improving in quality. Curricula have improved, new courses have been introduced, and programmes are less ideological than in the past.

There are more visiting foreign professors, exchange programmes and joint centres linked with overseas universities. China is also investing in a core group of elite universities such as Tsinghua, Beijing, Fudan and Nanjing universities, which it wants to be world class institutions.[71] This policy is already paying off: both Beijing and Tsinghua are now in the world's top 100 universities, and four or five others are rising up fast.[72] As a result, more students are willing to stay in China for postgraduate study than in the past.

To try and understand how attitudes are changing, we ran a focus group with four undergraduates from Tsinghua and six postgraduates from a CAS institute in Beijing. Wang Yong explained that he used to want to study abroad, but no longer felt it was necessary:

I can get everything I need here in China. If I stay, I will know more people here and have better connections. If I go abroad, I'll lose all of that. In terms of the quality of research you can do, the US is probably still the best place. But if you want to build a long-term career back in China, it's not always clear that going to the US is in your best interests. Some of the sea-turtles return and struggle to get a good job here.

Yet the attraction of the US remains strong. Zhao Kuoying, a biology undergraduate at Tsinghua, told us:

In my department, there are 99 of us graduating this year. Seventy of these will go to the US. Twenty will stay at Tsinghua. Two will go to Sweden, two to France. And five don't yet know what they will do. I'm one of those.

᎙᎙ ᎙᎙

The saying *'qiang da chutou niao'* – the bird that flies ahead gets shot down – is learnt early in life.

Despite the large graduate numbers that excite such attention in the West, some commentators suggest that China may still face a significant shortage of talent in certain areas.[73] As with scientific publications and citations, the figures can be used to tell different stories. Graduate numbers, in particular, tend to be wielded in a similar way to Mao-era steel output figures: they tell us something about size but nothing about quality. And despite the big numbers, it is clear that China cannot escape what *The Economist* has dubbed 'the battle for brainpower'.[74] A recent McKinsey survey found that only 10 per cent of Chinese graduates with seven years of experience are suited to jobs in a multinational company.[75] Such findings may be attributable to poor skills in English and a lack of the practical experience that large companies require, but they also suggest the need for further education reform.

Learning beyond the classroom

Traditions of rote learning, with their roots in the feats of brute memorisation required by the imperial examination system, are still remarkably pervasive. When Chinese pupils start school, their first task is to memorise thousands of characters, far more demanding than the 26 letters of the Roman alphabet. Pedagogical approaches that emphasise standard solutions for a predicted set of scenarios still dominate over interactive, problem-focused learning.

There can also be a tendency to prize conformity over difference. The saying *'qiang da chutou niao'* – the bird that flies ahead gets shot down – is learnt early in life. It inculcates a view that individuality is something to be kept in check, rather than a strength. While there is now infinitely more room for being individualistic than in the recent past, there are still limits. This is perhaps one reason why the lure of going overseas remains so strong. The US, in particular, is seen as a place where you can reinvent yourself, unencumbered by culture and tradition.

The multinational R&D managers that we interviewed had different views on the vexed question of creativity. Some didn't feel it was a huge problem, and could be addressed with adequate training. Others felt that even graduates from the best universities were poorly trained in lateral thinking and the type of joined-up management required in a global business environment. One mentioned that he ended up hiring his Chinese teacher because she had the quirky cast of mind he couldn't find in most of the ostensibly better-qualified candidates who made it through to interview.

The war for talent: views from the frontline

When people say to me, 'How far is China behind the US in terms of technology?,' I say 'three months if you don't count creativity'. If someone at MIT posts some results, then China can recreate it in three months. But it takes longer than that to train and instil creativity.
Harry Shum, Managing Director, Microsoft Research Asia

Creativity is a problem, especially when people start working here. Also a willingness to take responsibility and to show leadership. For example, at first, when I asked people to produce a research report, they would complete it but not put their name on it. They gave it to me as if I was the one who was then responsible for its contents. So I had to say, 'No, you need to take ownership of these ideas and put your name to them.' There are so many different cultural assumptions.
Christian Rehtanz, Director Corporate Research, ABB China

The Confucian tradition of respecting customs and hierarchy has cast a long shadow over modern China... Deference to authority and to existing paradigms is a major barrier to scientific breakthrough.
Mu-Ming Poo, Professor of Neurobiology, UC Berkeley and Director, CAS Institute of Neuroscience, Shanghai

Initiative and creativity can be a problem, especially with recent graduates, but it is changing slowly for the better. When we recruit graduates, at either Master's or PhD level, it takes about two years for them to work really effectively. If we recruit people who've studied or worked abroad, it's much quicker.
Ya Cai, Director, Unilever Research Centre, Shanghai

It's easy to find engineers. But finding the mid-level managers, the people who can grow talent and nurture the next level is very tricky. The fact that I'm sitting here talking to you in Shanghai is a sign of our failure to do that. But the problem really stems from the Chinese education system. It teaches you to follow instructions, but not to think on your feet. I'm more interested in the outsiders, those who are less conventional, who get left behind.
James Stanbridge, Director, Global Service Operations, Microsoft China

Growing numbers of returnees could help to accelerate the transformation of academic and workplace cultures. But their success is also ambiguous. The continued reluctance of many of the top tier of scientists and engineers to return is a further sign that the future of Chinese innovation will depend not on an inward-looking techno-nationalism, but on a cosmopolitanism that is open to flows of people and ideas. At the moment, with returnees often feeling that they are being kept at arm's length, it is not clear how open China is to more of these flows. To attract back the very best scientists will require further reform, both of the research system and of wider political culture. Creativity depends ultimately on openness and the freedom to debate and disagree.

But any foreign observers who doubt China's capacity for creativity would do well to spend an afternoon strolling around Dashanzi, the artistic district of Beijing which is a hothouse of experimentalism in film, art, music and animation. If the creativity and resourcefulness of Chinese scientists and engineers has been a critical factor in the dynamism of Silicon Valley over the past 20 years, it seems unlikely that these same qualities cannot be found in abundance within China itself. Further reform of the education and political system is needed, but with 1.3 billion brains to draw on, the prospects for Chinese innovation have never looked brighter.

4 Places
Regions on the rise

China

- Shenyang
- Beijing
- Dalian
- Tianjin
- Xi'an
- Chengdu
- Shanghai
- Wuhan
- Chongqing
- Guangzhou
- Shenzhen
- Hong Kong

Fusheng Pan is a man with a plan. After months of hard work, the deputy director-general of Chongqing Science and Technology Commission has just put the finishing touches to his province's science strategy. Its goal is to accelerate Chonqing's transition from a manufacturing zone into the high-tech hub of western China. By 2020, research will account for 2.5 per cent of GDP, and 60 per cent of economic growth will be derived from science and technology. Professor Pan smiles confidently: 'I believe Chongqing can enter the top eight of all Chinese provinces in terms of our scientific development.'[76]

Anything is possible. Stand still and Chongqing takes shape in front of your eyes. With 31 million inhabitants, Chongqing is the world's fastest-growing city. Over half a million people pour in each year from the countryside. James Kynge likens it to nineteenth-century Chicago, which was a gateway to the undeveloped lands of the west, where roads, railways and rivers converged.[77] Chongqing is in the same position today. It buffers the vast, rural expanse of western China at a time when the process of urbanisation is barely half complete. In 2007, roughly 400 million people live in China's towns and cities. By 2050 that number is expected to exceed one billion. Already, China has 90 cities with more than a million inhabitants. And as Jonathan Watts notes, while we have all heard of Beijing and Shanghai, 'the names of many others – Suqian, Suining, Xiantao, Xinghua, Liuan – are unfamiliar even to many Chinese'.[78]

58%

Just six cities – Beijing, Shanghai, Tianjin, Shenzhen, Shenyang and Guangzhou – produce 58 per cent of all invention patents.

All of which makes the urban and regional dimensions of Chinese innovation ever more critical. Progress in China over the past 20 years has been as much a story of local diversity as central control. Contrary to the idea that 'the world is flat', the reality, as Richard Florida has argued, is remarkably spiky:

In terms of both sheer economic horse power and cutting-edge innovation, surprisingly few regions truly matter in today's global economy. What's more, the tallest peaks… are growing ever higher, while the valleys mostly languish.[79]

In China, this phenomenon is acute. The three most innovative regions – the Yangtze River Delta (which includes Shanghai and 14 nearby cities), the Pearl River Delta (which includes Guangzhou, Shenzhen and Hong Kong) and the BoHai Rim (which includes Beijing and Tianjin) – account for just 3 per cent of China's land mass and 15 per cent of its population, but generate 45 per cent of GDP and over 70 per cent of international trade and investment.[80] Just six cities – Beijing, Shanghai, Tianjin, Shenzhen, Shenyang and Guangzhou – produce 58 per cent of all invention patents.[81] Particularly in Shanghai, R&D investment is surging ahead, and has already reached 2.5 per cent of GDP.[82] In some ways, the size of these regions makes it easier to think of them as equivalent to countries in their own right, similar in scale to Germany, France or the UK.

Go west
This spikiness means that the next phase of China's development will involve a struggle to spread the benefits of growth, especially to the rural west. In his annual address to the National People's Congress in March 2006, Prime Minister Wen Jiabao outlined what he described as a 'major historic task': the need to bridge the gaping divide between the cities and the countryside. Beijing is concerned that inequality will become a breeding ground for political unrest. In 2005, there were 87,000 protests and riots in rural areas, a fourfold increase in just ten years.

The Chinese government sees the accelerated development of cities such as Chongqing, which are bordered by rural hinterlands, as a top priority. This could mean shifting lower-cost manufacturing west, and allowing the eastern seaboard to focus on higher-value R&D. But Chongqing has innovation ambitions of its own. Its science budget is rising fast, and it now has an R&D workforce of around 60,000, and 74 research institutes, 16 of which are funded by central government. The jewels in its research crown include a team at Southwest University, which first sequenced the silkworm genome and published the results in *Science*.

In neighbouring Chengdu, part of Sichuan province, it is a similar story. 'You made a wise choice to visit Sichuan,' we were told by Tan Kailin at the local Science and Techology Commission. 'Of all the provinces in China, only two were invited to make presentations to the Science and Technology Congress in January: Sichuan and Shandong.'[83] R&D spending has grown by an average of 13 per cent each year since 2001, the highest levels in western China. Agricultural science and technology is a priority, as the province seeks ways of improving rural productivity. Other highlights include the National Engineering Research Centre for Biomaterials, which has been ranked as China's leading centre for biomaterials research, and Huaxi Medical School, which is in the top five medical schools. Zhang Xingdong, the director emeritus of the biomaterials centre, explained to us proudly that Sichuan has been selected to host the World Biomaterials Congress in 2012: 'the Olympics of biomaterials research'.[84]

A third significant cluster in the north-west is in Xi'an, the capital of Shaanxi province, which is home to one of China's largest software parks and a concentration of technical universities that produce over 30,000 software engineers each year.

Science applied
Richard Florida argues that one of the consequences of globalisation is that cities and regions find themselves competing for ever smaller niches, by mixing their talent and cost advantages in sophisticated ways.[85] In the south of China, what is most striking about the science and innovation strategies of Guangzhou and Shenzhen is how they plan to build on their existing niches, by concentrating less on basic science and more on its application to processing and manufacturing. Ma Xianmin, deputy director general of Guangdong Department of Science and Technology, admits:

We aren't necessarily trying to catch up in basic science. Beijing and Shanghai are likely to dominate that for some years to come. We will focus instead on the linkages between science, innovation and enterprise. A lot of the research from the rest of China is brought here to Guangdong to be commercialised.[86]

He emphasises that more than 70 per cent of the R&D personnel and 90 per cent of R&D expenditure in the province is within business, particularly large firms like Huawei and ZTE, which are based in Shenzhen and are now emerging as serious contenders in the global telecoms market.

In the same way, a variety of cities are developing distinctive niches, which may mean that the overall map of China's innovation system looks very different ten or 15 years from now. Potential hotspots worth watching include Dalian, Wuhan and Binhai New Area.

— *Dalian*
Located in the north-eastern province of Liaoning, Dalian is rapidly becoming one of China's main centres for software outsourcing. Most of its clients are Japanese firms, but with a talent pool of 800,000 trained IT professionals to draw on, it has clear ambitions to attract more business from the US and Europe. Dalian Software Park is the focus of much of this activity, with a growing range of companies specialising in software, business process outsourcing and IT services.[87]

— *Wuhan*
The capital of Hubei province, 400 miles west of Shanghai, Wuhan is particularly strong in optical electronics and transmission equipment. In 2000, an 'Optics Valley' project was launched, which aims to make Wuhan China's 'optoelectronics hub'. Since 2001, the number of patents filed from Wuhan has been growing by 40 per cent each year. There are 23 universities in the city, graduating 150,000 students each year.[88] Wuhan will also be the location of the first 'P4-level' laboratory in China, one of only a handful in the world, which will be capable of researching highly infectious diseases, such as Ebola, smallpox and avian influenza.[89]

The aim is for Binhai to have the same kind of catalysing effect in north-eastern China that Shenzhen had in the Pearl River Delta.

— *Binhai New Area*
Currently little more than a 90-mile strip of wasteland along China's northern coast, the Binhai New Area is a pet development project of President Hu Jintao and Prime Minister Wen Jiabao. In June 2006, they declared it an 'experimental zone for comprehensive reform', a status previously enjoyed only by the Pudong area of Shanghai. The aim is for Binhai to have the same kind of catalysing effect in north-eastern China that Shenzhen had in the Pearl River Delta. US$15 billion has been allocated for infrastructure projects over the next five years. Precisely what will be located there remains unclear, but high-tech R&D is likely to play a central role.

As the pattern of science and innovation across China changes, all that can be said with certainty is that surprising things are likely to emerge from surprising places. For a country like the UK, which currently has science and innovation representatives in five regions (Beijing, Shanghai, Guangzhou/Shenzhen, Chongqing and Hong Kong), the challenge is to keep scaling up our efforts, in order to gather intelligence and broker collaborations in these new and emerging centres.

Park life
Science and technology parks are another important feature of the landscape of Chinese innovation. The scale and speed of investment in these parks is unprecedented anywhere in the world. There are now 53 parks in operation across China, with 30 more planned by 2010.[90] Data from MOST shows that the turnover of the parks grew by almost 50 per cent year on year throughout the 1990s, to reach US$187 billion by 2002. In the same period, the number of people employed rose from 140,000 to almost 3.5 million.[91]

One of the most successful of these experiments is Zhongguancun Science Park (known as ZGC), sometimes called the 'Silicon Valley of China'. Spread across a large area of north-west Beijing, ZGC boasts the largest concentration of high-tech companies in China, and in 2002 generated revenues of US$29 billion. Its firms account for 40 per cent of China's software market and include the top internet portal Sina. It also houses a growing number of biotech and nanotech start-ups. The park benefits from its close proximity to Beijing and Tsinghua universities, and a number of top research institutes, and is sustained by dense networks of scientists, engineers and entrepreneurs, with numerous links zig-zagging back to the US, Europe, Taiwan and Korea.

The parks are clearly a success in terms of attracting investment, but how innovative are they? Science parks have become a key part of China's development orthodoxy; they reflect a willingness to think big and make serious investments in infrastructure. Yet, for now, the majority of firms within them still appear more focused on high-tech manufacturing than cutting-edge areas of R&D, and there is little evidence of cross-fertilisation between sectors and industries. Talking to park managers and tenants, compelling examples of successful innovation remain surprisingly hard to pin down. This may gradually change as part of the new drive for independent innovation, but for now it is tempting to agree with one assessment that 'conclusive empirical evidence of the advantages of a science park location has been elusive, and most findings suggest only marginal advantages at best'.[92]

Innovation sans frontières

Of course, getting the chemistry for innovation right in terms of people, places and ideas is far from straightforward. Driving through Zhangjiang Hi-Tech Park, considered by many to be the most successful park in China, one is immediately struck by the walls around the numerous companies, offices and research centres. The physical layout of the park is not very inspiring, or human in scale: the roads are long and set at right angles, and it can be hard to find anybody walking. The walls in particular create an impression of exclusion and inaccessibility.

Walls have played a crucial role in the history, culture and development of China. The Great Wall is the most obvious: over 5000 kilometres long and designed originally to keep out the 'barbarian' Mongolian hordes. There are also square walls around the Forbidden City in the centre of Beijing, and the second ring road is built on the site of the Beijing city wall, which was razed by Mao in the 1950s. Chinese companies, schools, hospitals and factories are always surrounded by walls: usually a square, with a gate, staffed by security guards in uniforms. Even a university like Tsinghua has a wall around it, with a front gate on one side and small gates on the other three sides. And walls now reach from the physical to the virtual world: the Chinese authorities attempt to police cyberspace with the so-called 'Great Firewall of China'. Julia Lovell writes that the construction of walls is 'a constant across Chinese history, an almost unthinking, undeniable cultural habit that China's rulers, and some of its people, seem unable and certainly unwilling to kick'.[93]

66 99

Can innovation flourish behind walls? Chinese walls are an enigma to foreign visitors. They suggest inwardness, secrecy and a lack of transparency.

Walls are significant because it is important in Chinese culture to delineate clearly what is inside and what is outside. Streets often have a suffix at the end, 'wai' outside, or 'nei' inside. It is always important to be clear whether something is inside and belongs, or outside and doesn't. Foreigners are 'laowai' (outsiders); Chinese from other parts of the country are 'waidiren' (folk from elsewhere).

Can innovation flourish behind walls? Chinese walls are an enigma to foreign visitors. They suggest inwardness, secrecy and a lack of transparency, and imply that openness and accessibility are restricted. Does the physical geography of how spaces for innovation are planned hint at underlying attitudes which may be limiting in other ways? There is no easy answer to this question, but it is a dynamic that those within China and outside can find themselves struggling with as they try to build effective networks for collaboration.

5 Business
Networks of innovation

'Will our success here in China mean less work in Sweden? It's a huge challenge to white-collar jobs. Not so much for our generation, but certainly for our children. But I also see the other side: that China needs more innovation to improve the quality of life here. So in many ways it's a good thing that it's happening so fast.'

Ralph Lofdahl, General Manager, Radio Network R&D Centre, Ericsson, Beijing

For Bert van den Bos, it all started with a holiday. In 2001, he visited Beijing and Shanghai for the first time: 'I was amazed by how hard-working, how ambitious people were, for themselves but also for China.' What he saw during his trip started him thinking, and when he returned to work as the head of Vodafone's R&D operations in the Netherlands, he began to explore with colleagues the possibility of Vodafone establishing an R&D centre in China. After a feasibility study, which compared China, India, Korea and Japan as potential R&D locations, they concluded that China was the obvious first choice. Vodafone already had a small office in Beijing, which it had opened in 2001 to coincide with the purchase of a 3.27 per cent stake in China Mobile Hong Kong. In 2004, Group R&D started to scope out in detail how an R&D centre might work. In 2005, Bert moved to Beijing for six months to put the final arrangements in place, and Vodafone's board gave its approval to the new centre in 2006.

Because of its stake in China Mobile, Vodafone doesn't have a consumer presence in China. This means that its motivations for doing R&D are different from those of many companies. As Bert explains:

Doing R&D in China is often seen as a way of building a market, or gaining favour with the government. We are there because we expect a lot of innovations in wireless and mobile to flow from major vendors like Huawei and ZTE and also from Chinese start-ups over the next five or ten years. We want to build alliances with the right people and bring the next generation of Chinese technologies to Europe. So for us, this is about much more than marketing.

Vodafone is now hiring its first group of Chinese engineers, and plans for the centre to be fully operational by the autumn of 2007. First, these new recruits will be brought to Europe for six months to learn more about Vodafone's corporate culture, and to build good working relationships with colleagues from elsewhere in the business. Such an intensive training programme is not cheap, but once the centre is up and running, Bert estimates that the costs per engineer will be around two-thirds of those in the UK. By the end of 2007, the ambition is to have a team of 20 in Beijing, rising to 50 during 2009. This will represent an investment of around 12% of Vodafone's total R&D spend. Bert is keen to emphasise 'this is additional money – not the result of offshoring our R&D from Europe'. But he says that long-term plans still need to be decided:

As it is early days for us it is still not clear how much might move to China in the long term. The assessment we have made is that there won't be a big shift within five years. Beyond that it's hard to say.[94]

R&D heads east
Vodafone is one of a rising number of foreign companies locating their R&D in China. Motorola was the first to open an R&D lab back in 1993, followed by a handful of pioneers in the late 1990s such as Microsoft and Nokia. But in the past three years there has been a noticeable spike in the number of multinational R&D centres.[95] By the end of 2005, the Chinese Ministry of Commerce put the total at around 750. This figure needs to be treated with some caution, as it includes centres doing product adaptation for the Chinese market, as well as those doing more innovative, global-facing R&D. As Sylvia Schwaag Serger points out, some centres were also opened as a way of improving relations or clinching deals with the Chinese government. Others 'exist more on paper than in reality' having been announced with a fanfare long before they are fully operative.[96]

Yet despite these caveats, there is no denying the growing significance of China as an R&D location. Schwaag Serger puts the number of multinational centres at closer to 250, and suggests that around 60 of these are 'performing innovative R&D activities'. We interviewed several of the managers of these centres, including ABB, AstraZeneca, Ericsson, Intel, Microsoft, Sun Microsystems and Unilever. The box below details some of the reasons they gave for locating in China.

When I came to China, I discovered that one particular technology which we'd developed was already here. Someone had copied it, and it was quite widely available. We didn't even realise it was here... We hadn't kept track of who was doing what here, or what was being published in Chinese journals. We urgently needed experts who could follow these things for us.
Christian Rehtanz, director of corporate research, ABB Beijing R&D Centre[97]

At first, the research we were doing was related to market access. But to be honest, we've found it even more cost effective to do R&D here than I thought was possible. The speed with which we can develop prototypes is key. The turnaround is so fast that even if the quality is a little lower, we get them so quickly that we can have many more attempts at getting them right. We get more shots at the same problem for a lower cost.
Ralph Lofdahl, general manager, Radio Network R&D Center[98]

Decisions about where to locate manufacturing are relatively easy. It's now a science, with established methodologies. But locating R&D is more of an art. For Intel, our top factors are: 1) people; 2) people; 3) people; 4) customers; 5) government.
Mark Griffin, head of PRC Digital Enterprise Group, Intel[99]

Lower costs are still a factor, but not as much as they were. It's more about being close to where the market is growing fastest... Availability of talent is also key. Our labs in Europe are finding it harder to recruit in certain areas; there's a noticeable tightening of availability. And there's also the use of TCM [traditional Chinese medicine] to generate new products. We are now just one step away from TCM-based products being launched on the global market.
Ya Cai, director, Unilever Research China[100]

As these quotes suggest, while R&D costs remain substantially lower in China than in Europe, this is no longer the main factor in location decisions. New facilities are opening each month, often prompted by a desire to reach and respond to a growing Chinese domestic market. Sectors such as pharmaceuticals are set to grow rapidly, with Novartis, AstraZeneca and GSK all announcing plans to scale up their R&D.[101] Frank Yuan of AstraZeneca predicts:

Within five years, all of the global top ten pharma companies will have R&D facilities in China. It's moving incredibly fast. You'll have to update your report on this within six months.[102]

Apart from looking to China's top universities as a source of recruits, multinational centres appear relatively detached from the rest of China's innovation system. As in India, some critics voice concerns about multinationals absorbing the best talent, and the absence of measurable spill-over effects within Chinese industry, combined with the new focus on indigenous innovation, has led some to speculate that there could be a backlash against multinational R&D. Dr Lan Xue of the School of Public Policy and Management at Tsinghua University argues that 'R&D centres need to build stronger links with local universities and institutions, so they can help to build capacity rather than just drain it away'.[103]

Homegrown giants?

China's innovation system has been good at supporting some high-class research institutes (largely under CAS), as well as a handful of excellent universities. But R&D within Chinese enterprises has long been an area of weakness. Links between universities, research institutes and companies have been poor, and companies have not prioritised investment in R&D. The focus on indigenous innovation in the new 15-year plan aims to create policy and institutional frameworks that get innovation moving. As Shang Yong, the vice minister of MOST, recently observed: 'We can't have technological innovation without institutional innovation.'

There is also an aspiration to have more globally competitive Chinese firms. With the exception of oil and gas companies such as PetroChina and CNOOC, few Chinese companies have made a big impact on global markets. This is starting to change, as names such as Huawei, Lenovo and Haier become more familiar overseas. As table 5 suggests, there is now a clutch of Chinese brands that could have a global reach within five to ten years.

Table 5 Top ten Chinese global brands

1	Lenovo	6	Tsingtao Brewery
2	Haier	7	CCTV
3	Bank of China	8	CNOOC
4	Air China	9	Huawei
5	China Mobile	10	Ping An

Source: *Financial Times*/McKinsey survey; see R McGregor, 'China's companies count down to lift off', *Financial Times*, 30 Aug 2005

China's largest high-tech firms, such as Huawei and Lenovo (which in December 2004 acquired IBM's PC division), do appear to be prioritising research and development. Huawei now has R&D centres in Bangalore, Dallas, San Diego, Amsterdam, Stockholm and Moscow, as well as 10,000 research staff in China. Ten per cent of its turnover is now allocated to R&D and it is the only Chinese firm to feature on the World Intellectual Property Organization's list of the 50 most innovative global firms. ZTE follows close behind, as China's second largest telecoms equipment firm. Other companies investing significantly in R&D include Sina and Sohu, China's largest web portals; Shanda, the online gaming provider; and Huaqi, which makes MP3 players under its Aigo brand and has 200 of its 1500 staff in R&D.

Yet these companies remain the exception in a country where business R&D is still relatively underdeveloped. There are a variety of reasons for this: Chinese firms are often very hierarchical and dominated by their founders, so there can be a tendency not to take initiative and to defer to senior management. Firms also tend to rush into unrelated business activities, rather than make investments on the basis of strategic planning. Added to this, ownership is often a thorny issue. While firms may claim to be private, the state often maintains a share, or is able to favour the company through special relationships and arrangements such as preferential loans, market access or tax breaks. The boundary between public and private can be quite hazy. This can give rise to ambiguities about the level of state influence in company decision-making, of the type that undermined CNOOC's attempt in 2005 to buy the US oil firm UNOCAL.[104]

Yet as always in China, it can be easy to look in the wrong place, and read the wrong signs. We may be mistaken to concentrate only on the handful of large firms that have already gained some international visibility. Denis Simon, the veteran observer of Chinese science policy, suggests that small- and medium-sized enterprises (SMEs) are more likely to be the 'volcano' that erupts and changes the landscape of Chinese innovation.[105] Until now, many SMEs have been constrained by a lack of access to capital or stock market listing. Policies for indigenous innovation aim to change this and support small firms to grow through investment in R&D.

Intellectual property tightens up

In February 2006, Netac, a small data storage company in Shenzhen, became embroiled in a legal battle over patent infringement with a US rival, PNY Technologies. Such cases are common in China, where weak enforcement of intellectual property laws has long been a problem. On this occasion, though, it was the Chinese firm suing its American rival. Jeff Xiang, the vice president of Netac, explains why they had to go down this route:

We tried to talk to PNY about licensing fees for our technology. But they weren't interested. So we were forced to resort to the courts in the US to protect our rights. We're just trying to make sure everyone plays by the same rules.[106]

Netac's readiness to defend its intellectual property may be a sign of what is to come, as more Chinese firms invest in patents and have a strong interest in enforcing them. Such examples complicate the picture of China as, in Ted Fishman's words:

a counterfeit economy... in which the vast majority of goods branded as one thing are made by someone else. Everything from simply copied commodity products... to goods higher up the economic and technical food chain such as biotechnology, automotive and aerospace products all have their unofficial knockoffs.[107]

10%

IP 'rights' are generally of good quality and cost around 10 per cent of their equivalents in most G8 countries.

Ian Harvey, chairman of the Intellectual Property Institute, argues that foreign observers have become so locked into a cycle of complaining about intellectual property (IP) in China that they are in danger of missing the improvements of recent years. He points out that there are three components to an effective IP regime: the underpinning law, the cost and quality of the patent 'right' acquired, and the effectiveness and cost of enforcing that right. Against each of these criteria, China now performs well: following a series of measures, its legal infrastructure 'is among the best in the world'; IP 'rights' are generally of good quality and cost around 10 per cent of their equivalents in most G8 countries; and enforcement through the courts is also cheap and takes little more than a year, compared with five to seven years in the US.[108]

Counterfeiting is still a problem, but Harvey says that there is a need to distinguish between this and patent infringement: 'Just because you can buy fake bags and DVDs in Silk Street market it doesn't mean that the whole system is deficient.'[109] Although the quality of enforcement can still vary across the country, almost 250,000 cases of IP infringement were brought in 2005, more than in any other country. Over 90 per cent of foreign companies taking legal action in China win their cases, compared with between 30 and 40 per cent in the US. Outside the big players in the FTSE 100, Harvey worries that the senior managers of many British companies fail to understand how IP in China works, and so miss the significance of these changes. He notes that British companies file far fewer patents in China than are filed by Germany, the Netherlands, Sweden or Switzerland.

Often, the problems that companies experience in China are of their own making. They haven't invested the time and resources needed to understand how to enforce their IP, and then they complain loudly when it all goes wrong.[110]

Harvey is right to highlight the significant improvements in China's IP regime. Nonetheless, others would argue that he is too optimistic given more persistent weaknesses in China's legal system (for example, over the appointment of judges) which undermine IP enforcement as much as other aspects of the rule of law.

Setting new standards

In parallel with these improvements to its IP regime, China is increasingly using the process of setting technical standards as a way of strengthening its domestic firms. In sectors such as mobile telecoms and nanotechnology, influencing the technical standards that are adopted internationally can be an important way of shaping future markets. Examples of China's efforts in this regard include the WAPI standard for wireless internet access, which was proposed as an alternative to the widely used 802.11x 'wi-fi' standard; the TD-SCDMA standard for third-generation mobile telephony; new standards for remote-frequency identification and product tracking (RFID); and next-generation internet protocols.[111]

This more ambitious standards strategy has been received warily outside China. WAPI, in particular, was the subject of a sharp diplomatic row with the US. Yet, as Richard Suttmeier and colleagues argue in a thoughtful paper for the National Bureau of Asian Research, 'given its market size, cultural preferences, and growing technological capabilities, China will be active in standard-setting for the long term'.[112] The question for Europe and the US is what form this activism will take. China will naturally promote its interests through the standards process, but it must avoid pursuing a crude techno-nationalist approach, which could backfire and leave it isolated in relation to certain new technologies. At the same time, the international community must show greater 'sensitivity to Chinese concerns over the distributive consequences and procedural fairness of global standards practices'.[113]

The bottom line

The contribution of business and enterprise to China's innovation system is evolving fast. At the moment, multinational R&D centres are attracting a lot of attention, but there are fewer of these doing cutting-edge global research than official data would suggest. They will remain an eye-catching feature of the innovation landscape, but their significance in terms of wider effects on the innovation system is probably exaggerated.

More interesting are the changes under way within Chinese companies. From a very low base, there are signs of a pick-up in business R&D. This is most obvious in the handful of large firms that enjoy strong government backing: Lenovo, Huawei, ZTE and Haier. The crucial question is whether SMEs can fulfil their potential to become what Xu Guanhua, China's science minister, describes as the 'birthing cribs' of larger, more innovative companies.[114] This is the challenge at the heart of the new 15-year plan, and it remains to be seen whether it can be met.

For a long time, winning a Nobel Prize has been seen as the summit of China's scientific ambition.[115] This is now joined by another goal: to have at least 50 Chinese companies in the Fortune Global 500 by 2020.[116]

6 Culture
Myths of the wild east

'Will China have the same kind of case as Hwang? Definitely, yes. But where? We don't know. The question is will we have the courage to discover and expose it?'

Professor Hu Chingli, Shanghai Jiaotong University, speech during the Opening Plenary of the World Bioethics Congress, Beijing, 6 Aug 2006

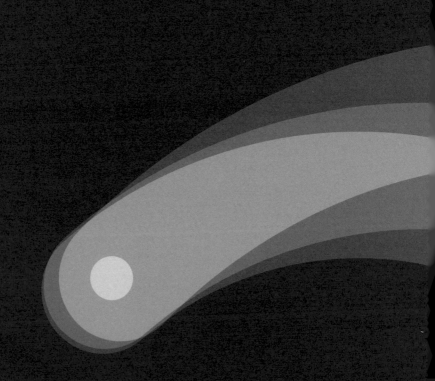

On 6 August 2006, the World Bioethics Congress opened in Beijing. Professor Renzong Qiu took to the podium to address the first plenary session. The contrast with a similar event eight years earlier could not have been more marked. Then, during the 1998 World Congress of the International Genetics Federation, many delegates had stayed at home following a boycott campaign centred on China's eugenics and family planning policies. In 2006, over 600 bioethicists turned up, including many of the most eminent names in the field. These different responses reflect just how far China has come in its approach to these debates.

Nonetheless, some commentators still portray China as a 'wild east', where the onward march of scientific progress is unconstrained by ethical qualms or public unease. There are fears that a lack of transparency and problems of regulatory enforcement, combined with large amounts of funding for scientists who are under pressure to generate results, can lead to ethical shortcuts. Critics also argue that individual rights are not sufficiently respected in China, resulting in dubious research practices. One prominent example occurred in Henan, in a drug trial with HIV-positive villagers. Villagers signed up for unapproved trials at Ditan Hospital in Beijing using drugs supplied by Viral Genetics from California.[117] Patients allegedly suffered side effects, and later complained that they had signed forms without being told what the trial was for. When they asked to see the forms, they were told they had to pay for them.

Renzong Qiu acknowledges that occasionally there can be a 'wildness' to scientific research in China. But, he says, we should not allow high-profile incidents of ethical misconduct to obscure the ongoing efforts by policy-makers and bioethicists to develop new regulations and comply with international guidelines. We must also avoid judging China by impossible standards: 'even in the "civilised" west, sometimes scientists will degenerate into wildness'.[118] Rather than framing these debates in terms of 'east' and 'west', he argues instead for greater respect and understanding to be shown by all sides in ethical dialogue.

Hubris and hybrids

Professor Qiu is right to highlight the progress China has made in relation to scientific and medical ethics over the past decade, often by adopting regulations modelled on those found in the UK and the US. For example, in 2003, the Ministry of Health (MOH) issued new guidelines on human embryonic stem cell research, and in 2006 it proposed new regulations for biomedical research on human subjects. China has also played an important role in global agreements such as the UNESCO Universal Declaration on the Human Genome and Human Rights (1998) and the Helsinki Declaration on Ethical Principles for Medical Research involving Human Subjects (2000).

Yet while this engagement on the international stage is encouraging, there are still concerns about what happens inside China. The general view is that, while the MOH has shown some interest, it has been an uphill struggle to get ethical concerns addressed in the major scientific programmes led by MOST, such as 863 and 973. Significantly, there is scant mention of ethics in the new 15-year plan. Renzong Qiu recalls how

in 2000, I drafted an ethical and social strand for the 863 programme, but when this was sent to MOST, the minister said the time wasn't yet right to address such issues, so they delayed the whole thing... It's not that they think the issues are unimportant. The Hwang case in Korea has obviously created quite a stir. But even though budgets for science are rising fast, there's very little funding for bioethics research.[119]

As with many issues in China, even where regulations exist, it is not clear that there are adequate mechanisms to implement them. At the World Congress on Bioethics, some of the Chinese delegates suggested that because regulations are issued by the MOH, rather than the State Council, it is not clear that they apply to all researchers. One argued: 'We need an ethics advisory committee in the premier's office, not only for stem cells but for other new technologies. If only MOH issues guidelines it is difficult to control the situation.'[120] Another senior biologist complained: 'Bioethics are still not being built into science courses or even PhDs. The courses are extremely narrow and ethics don't even feature.'

Difficulties in making the rules work are also reflected in the system of institutional review boards (IRBs), which are supposed to review ethical dilemmas and advise on good practice. These boards are often chaired by the head of the research institute or hospital concerned, which can lead to conflicts of interest. Board members have only limited training in research ethics, and rarely include professional bioethicists. The net effect, according to one researcher, is that 'IRBs are like a rubber stamp. There is no discussion. There are no suggestions, no revisions, no rejections.'[121]

This points to the need for more capacity-building in China around bioethics. Some argue that more effort is required to train scientists in internationally agreed bioethical concepts and practices. Others call for more thinking about what a distinctively Chinese bioethics might look like, drawing on Confucianism and Daoism.

The public value of science

Sheila Jasanoff has described how bioethical debates can become either elitist, when they are tacked on to existing technocratic regulatory cultures, or more deliberative, when they create opportunities for scientists and the wider public to reflect on the aims and purposes of science.[122] In China, public participation is an increasingly important theme in political life, and there are cautious experiments taking place in many areas. To what extent science and innovation are included in these remains to be seen. Until now, bioethics has been regarded mainly as an intellectuals' project, rather than a set of questions for wider societal discussion.

" **"**

I think we urgently need a wider debate in Chinese society about where science is taking us, what it's for.
Renzong Qiu

Alongside the 15-year plan, several new initiatives have been announced to improve levels of scientific literacy.[123] Various organisations have been set up to support these efforts, such as the China Institute of Science Popularisation, and a National Science Popularisation Day has been established (4 July). There is no end of community science exhibitions, museums and websites disseminating information.

Yet these activities often seem to be directed towards a perceived public-information deficit, and have a supply-side feel, with echoes of the Communist Party's mass campaigns. As Renzong Qiu observes, there is still a long way to go before China develops the more open, two-way forms of dialogue between science and society that are now commonplace in Europe:

The scientists themselves have a vision, a sense of where their work might be taking us. But they don't open this up for discussion. Their views are expressed in closed rooms. When new programmes are developed, there's no debate involving the public – or even intellectuals. I think we urgently need a wider debate in Chinese society about where science is taking us, what it's for.[124]

Policing misconduct

If frameworks for bioethics are steadily improving, one problem that appears to be worsening across Chinese science is that of plagiarism and research fraud. While nothing has so far attracted the international notoriety of the Woo-Suk Hwang affair in South Korea, the past two years have seen a series of minor scandals over research ethics. The highest profile case involved Jin Chen, dean of the Microelectronics School at Shanghai Jiaotong University, who was fired in May 2006 for faking the research behind a supposedly groundbreaking microchip. Dr Chen, who had received government praise for his work and was the recipient of over £7.5 million in research grants, was discovered to have been reusing chips made by one of Motorola's subsidiaries, to which he had simply added his company logo.[125]

2006

In May 2006, an 'open letter on research integrity' was signed by 120 Chinese scientists mostly working in the US.

Dr Chen was eventually caught after a whistleblower reported him to the university authorities. There is concern though about the many cases that go unreported, and the wider climate of research misconduct that some feel is being fostered by the incentives and evaluation procedures now in place across the Chinese research system. It is easy to pin the blame on the moral weakness of individual scientists, while ignoring the wider reasons why such cases occur. Dr Chen is a case in point. He received a substantial salary to return to China from the US, and a big grant for his research. But with such largesse comes regular scrutiny of results and an assessment system that can be unforgiving of those who fail. Misconduct is an almost inevitable product of this mix. Another is stress and even suicide: there has been a spate of deaths among young Chinese scientists in the past two years, linked to the intense pressures of research assessment.[126] As one PhD student told us:

There are so many pressures and inducements, so many temptations. Money, power and prestige all flow from scientific success. But there shouldn't be so much pressure on scientists at such an early stage in their careers.[127]

Behind these more extreme examples, there is a more subtle and pervasive culture of plagiarism within higher education. In a recent interview with *Science*, Ouyang Zhingcan, director of CAS's Institute of Theoretical Physics, described an environment 'that's rife with simultaneous or serial duplicate manuscript submissions, self-plagiarized cookie-cutter papers, individual and institutional honorary authorship, and outright plagiarism'.[128] Policy-makers are waking up to these problems, particularly after the Hwang affair, which has sensitised many to the ease with which a country's scientific reputation can be tarnished. There has also been pressure applied from elsewhere. In May 2006, an 'open letter on research integrity' was signed by 120 Chinese scientists mostly working in the US and sent to Xu Guanhua, the minister for science. It called for new procedures to prevent misconduct and compulsory courses for students and researchers on research integrity and scientific ethics.[129] In November 2006, MOST responded to these calls by announcing a series of measures, including the creation of a special office for research integrity within MOST, tough new penalties for plagiarism and falsifying data, and a tightening up of the system for project evaluation.[130]

It will take time for these policies to have an effect. Some, however, remain sceptical that the changes will be adequate to tackle the root causes of misconduct. Shi-min Fang, a biochemist and science writer based in San Diego, is an influential voice in these debates. In 1994, he launched the Chinese-language website New Threads,[131] which has exposed around 500 cases of research fraud in recent years. His efforts have not been without controversy, with some accusing New Threads of circulating unjustified rumours, but Shi-min Fang is clear about the service that the site provides:

[It] is playing a limited but essential role in fighting corruption in Chinese science for two reasons: First, China does not have [a] free press... Second, there is not a credible official channel to report, investigate and punish scientific misconduct. The cheaters don't have to worry they will someday be caught and punished. Therefore the misconduct becomes rampant.

He accepts that these issues are now moving up the policy agenda, but feels that the government is 'just paying lip service to this issue. Although some guidelines have been created, they are rarely enforced.'[132]

Ethical alliances

Research cultures in China are being pulled in different directions. In some areas, such as the regulation of biomedical science, concerted efforts are under way to both meet and help shape international ethical standards. Media myths of a scientific 'wild east' may be hard to dispel, but the robustness of many of the policies that are being put in place shows that China wants to make a serious contribution to the governance of global science. As well as learning from good practices abroad, China has rich philosophical and cultural resources of its own to bring to these processes of ethical reflection.

At the same time, enforcing high standards across China's science and innovation system remains a challenge, and is made more difficult by regular incidents of research fraud and plagiarism. Rumbles of disquiet about misconduct could erupt at any point into a larger Hwang-style scandal. MOST is introducing new measures to prevent this, despite the fact that it is government policies and incentives that are in many ways the cause of the problem. The pressures being placed on most Chinese researchers to generate papers and other outputs make the UK's research assessment exercise look positively benign. This will make eradicating misconduct a prolonged and difficult task.

All of this suggests the need for more and better alliances between Chinese scientists, ethicists and policy-makers and their counterparts overseas. Governance and ethics are under-explored dimensions in the comparative analysis of innovation systems. In UK and European policy discussions, it is sometimes argued that devoting too much attention to these questions will 'hold us back', while Asia forges ahead, less encumbered by such concerns. We need partnerships to demonstrate how the opposite argument can apply. Evidence from the environmental sphere suggests that countries can gain competitive advantage from the adoption of higher standards, which stimulate alternative innovation pathways.[133] In the same way, a more proactive UK or European stance on issues of ethics and governance could attract new collaborators who want to help develop these frameworks and participate in cosmopolitan networks of innovation. For example, a number of the stem cell researchers we interviewed in China said that one of the factors that made collaboration with the UK attractive was its high-quality regulatory and ethical framework for research.

BIONET: Cooperation in the ethical governance of research

The EU-funded BIONET project is a new type of ethical alliance. It brings together scientists, social scientists and practitioners from China and Europe to exchange ideas and develop shared approaches to the governance of biomedicine. The goal of the network is to support joint research, inform policy, and build the capacity of participants to address the ethical questions raised by their work. Nikolas Rose, the coordinator of BIONET, says that they plan to start by looking at two areas: stem cell research and pharmacogenetics. Attempts to harmonise ethical frameworks should not, he argues, involve 'the unitary imposition of European values on China at the expense of its own ethical traditions and culture'.[134]

New alliances may also be required to discourage multinational firms from exploiting different ethical frameworks by moving controversial research offshore. For example, we visited a number of animal testing facilities that are actively marketing their services to western companies. One, in Chengdu, boasted in its glossy brochure of 'four beagle dog rooms, six monkey rooms, two rabbit rooms, two animal labs… for domestic and overseas clients'.[135] The ethical rights and wrongs of this are debatable; however, some European companies clearly feel it makes sense to outsource animal testing to Chengdu, given regulatory hurdles and public opposition at home. Nonetheless, some form of ethical oversight is clearly important, particularly when the services on offer go beyond animal testing to include human clinical trials. Global businesses are well used to the challenges of managing their manufacturing supply chains in a socially responsible way. As R&D networks become increasingly global, these same challenges will apply to the supply chain for research.

7 Collaboration
Positive sum games

'I do not believe that in the next stage of the global economy, success for one country need mean failure on the part of the other. Globalisation is not a zero sum game where one country or continent will only succeed at the expense of another.'

Gordon Brown MP, Chancellor of the Exchequer, speech at the Chinese Academy of Social Sciences, 21 Feb 2005

Science and technology have long played a central role in Sino–British relations. As the historian Julia Lovell recounts in her book *The Great Wall*, the first British trade mission to China, despatched by King George III in September 1792, carried with it 'the most impressive fruits of recent technological progress – telescopes, clocks, barometers, airguns and, naturally, a hot-air balloon – all intended to dazzle the Chinese emperor, Qianlong, into opening trade with the West.'[136] Sadly, Qianlong remained unmoved. 'We have never valued ingenious articles,' he wrote to Lord Macartney who led the British mission, 'nor do we have the slightest need of your country's manufactures.'[137]

Today there is a more positive tone to scientific exchanges between Britain and China. Between January 2005 and March 2006, the two nations ran a 'Partners in Science' programme that comprised over 140 events designed to raise awareness and promote research collaboration. The outcomes of the year include projects on climate change and e-science. A team from the UK's Medical Research Council is also working with China's National Centre for Drug Screening to identify compounds active against malaria.[138]

The rules of attraction

Science has always been an international undertaking, so as the production and application of scientific knowledge becomes more globalised, we should expect networks of collaboration to spread and intensify. A recent survey by the UK Office of Science and Innovation found that 73 per cent of British universities expect their international engagement to increase over the next decade.[139] More collaboration will bring a number of benefits: it can provide access to knowledge and expertise that may not be available locally; it can increase the international reach and impact of research; it can open up new markets and business opportunities; and it can enable large science projects to be undertaken at scale.[140]

Between Britain and China, a huge amount of joint activity already takes place, much of it driven from the bottom up by the enthusiasm and networking of individual scientists. Flows of students and researchers are also strong.[141]
Yet as China's investment in science grows and its innovation system matures, the question for Britain is whether we need to do more, to scale up the level and ambition of our collaborative efforts in ways that can benefit both countries.

Some examples of China–UK collaboration

In September 2006, **Leeds University** and the **Chinese Academy of Sciences** announced a **virtual joint laboratory**, funded in part by the UK's Biotechnology and Biological Sciences Research Council (BBSRC). Plant scientists from Leeds and agricultural specialists from CAS will work on joint projects in the field of rice genomics, aiming to understand how plants react to environmental stress and high salt levels.

Launched in 2003, the **China–UK Cambridge (CUC) Venture Park** helps Chinese companies to expand their markets and develop research links in the UK. It is backed by the Guangzhou municipal government and targets companies from that region. In 2007, it will concentrate its networking activities on biotechnology and traditional Chinese medicine.

Around 1000 students are now enrolled at **Nottingham Ningbo University**, the first foreign-run university campus in China. The aim is to have 4000 undergraduates by 2008. Established as a partnership between Nottingham and China's Wani Education Group, this £35 million (500 million RMB) campus is an innovative attempt by a UK university to win a share of China's expanding education market.

Some examples of China–UK collaboration cont.

In September 2006, Tony Blair and Wen Jiabao launched **Innovation China UK** (ICUK), which aims to help Chinese and UK universities commercialise joint research. With £5 million from the UK Higher Education Innovation Fund, and equivalent support from MOST, the project will finance the commercialisation of near-market technologies. 'There are umpteen collaborations going on with China. What I'm interested in is getting a real return on that investment,' says Caroline Quest, managing director of innovation and enterprise at Queen Mary, University of London, who is coordinating the project.[142]

Around 3000 plant species grow on the Jade Dragon Snow Mountain in China's Yunnan Province. Studying and preserving this biodiversity is the focus of **The Lijiang Project**, set up by the Royal Botanic Garden Edinburgh, the Kunming Institute of Botany and the Yunnan Academy of Agricultural Science. One of the project's main activities is the Jade Dragon Field Station, which opened in 2004 as the UK's first joint scientific laboratory in China.

Existing collaborations typically fall into one of five categories:

— *Multilateral programmes and projects*, which involve more than two countries and are often designed to tackle major global scientific challenges. Examples include the Human Genome Project, which had 20 partners and a budget of €2 billion, and ITER (the proposed International Thermonuclear Experimental Reactor), a €10 billion collaboration between the EU, Japan, China, India, South Korea, Russia and the US. The Framework Programmes of the EU are another important mechanism, which allow research teams in 'third countries', including China, to receive funding for joint research. Under Framework 6, China was the second largest non-EU recipient of funding, with around €900 million of research spread across 130 projects.[143] These opportunities will expand further under Framework 7, which runs from 2007 to 2013, and has a total budget of €53 billion.

— *Multinational corporate R&D*, which involves individual companies establishing research links with companies, universities or research institutes in China. Examples include the Tsinghua–BP Clean Energy Research Centre, which the oil giant established with Tsinghua University in 2003; and the Beijing-1 satellite, developed from a partnership between Surrey Satellite Technology and MOST.[144]

— *Bilateral programmes or centres*, which are funded by the Chinese and partner governments, or by research councils in both countries. Both the French and German governments have set up several joint centres that fall into this category, and some Franco–German science bodies have done likewise, including the Institut Pasteur, which in 2004 opened a branch in Shanghai, and the Max Planck Society, which runs a centre with CAS. Large initiatives of this type are rarely established by the UK, although individual research councils sometimes run targeted schemes, such as the Engineering and Physical Sciences Research Council (EPSRC) 'Interact' scheme, which recently allocated £750,000 to UK collaborations with China, India or Japan.[145]

— *Bottom-up networking and joint research*, which covers a vast range of activities from attendance at conferences to joint projects and co-authored papers. Much of this activity is not directly funded, but supported from existing grants that each partner holds. Larger projects may also apply for funding through the normal responsive mode, with research councils on each side supporting their country's participation. So, for example, a nanoscientist at Cambridge University might apply to do a project with a nanoscientist in a CAS laboratory, with EPSRC covering the UK costs and the NSFC covering the Chinese side. In addition, there are many formal and informal institutional links between UK/European and Chinese universities and institutes, which may become the basis for more substantive collaboration.

— *Research fellowships and travel scholarships*, which support students, postgraduates and more experienced scientists to study or spend time abroad. These are a crucial way of building networks that can sustain other forms of collaboration over the long term. Most European countries operate their own schemes: one of the most successful is that run by the Humboldt Foundation in Germany, which has so far graduated over 20,000 scientists and 35 Nobel Prize winners.[146] The European Union also runs a substantial programme in the form of the Marie Curie fellowships.[147] UK schemes include the Chevening Scholarships, which in 2004/05 brought 2124 scholars to the UK (of which 277 were from China, the largest country group); the Dorothy Hodgkin Postgraduate Awards, which support around 100 PhD applicants each year from China, India, South Africa, Brazil and Russia to study at UK universities; and the Scholarships for Excellence programme, which has an annual budget of £840,000, and in 2007 will support 50 Chinese PhD and postdoctoral students to attend Oxford, Cambridge, Manchester, Edinburgh or Nottingham universities.[148]

In order to get a better understanding of how individual European countries are approaching collaboration, we interviewed the science counsellors at several embassies in Beijing, and talked to the directors of a handful of bilateral research centres. The box below details some of their observations on the value of their collaborations.

As I see it, we have a 15-year window to set up partnerships and become a real technology player in China before they won't need us, they can just do it on their own. So you're either inside doing something or you're outside... People often ask shouldn't we stay at home and keep our best knowledge in Helsinki? But I don't think that's an option.
Jaani Heinonen, Science Counsellor, FinnChi Innovation Center, Shanghai[149]

I think eventually new schemes will be developed that don't replace the bottom-up model, but co-exist alongside it. This already happens to some extent: Galileo, ITER are top down... Until now, there's been little discussion within the EU about which areas we should collaborate on with China. And this has been to China's advantage. It's been able to play off different EU members against one another, by encouraging lots of different bilateral collaborations. But under Framework 7, there are 35 key technology platforms, which we could at least start using to identify which fields and subfields are of importance... Suddenly the EU could find itself becoming a lot more coordinated, a lot more strategic.
Georges Papageorgiou, Minister Counsellor, Science and Technology, European Commission, Beijing[150]

I am quite critical of the European Commission in this area. Too often it acts as a separate country, as a separate member state, rather than as a representative of all EU members. It would be very difficult to channel more activity through the EU because we all approach science funding so differently.
Dr Hartmut Keune, Science Counsellor, German Embassy, Beijing[151]

Over and above the approaches of different EU member states, there are substantial amounts of collaboration and flows of researchers between China and the US, Japan, Australia and Canada.[152] Also significant is the expanding nexus of bilateral linkages between China and India. In September 2006, the two countries agreed to set up a ministerial-level steering committee to promote scientific cooperation.[153] If the UK and Europe are not willing or able to scale up their collaboration with China, plenty of other countries are queuing up to take their place.

Britain's asset base

Yet it is wrong to see this as a game in which one side holds all the cards. The UK's science and innovation system has many strengths which make it attractive to China. With just 1 per cent of the world's population, the UK produces 9 per cent of all scientific papers and receives 12 per cent of citations.[154] It is also home to two of the world's top ten universities, and six of the best across Europe.[155] This reputation for academic excellence means that the UK is popular with international students. One recent survey of 28,000 prospective students across 50 countries placed the UK second only to the US as an education destination of choice.[156]

These factors are reflected in the data on levels of China–UK collaboration. In terms of talent flows, the total number of Chinese studying in UK universities rose sharply from 6310 in 1999/2000 to 52,675 in 2004/05, of which 28,170 are postgraduates.[157] The rate of growth has slowed in the past two years but, on any measure, the UK is still a top destination for Chinese students. Only the US attracts more – around 65,000 in 2005.[158]

The picture is also positive in relation to co-authored publications. New analysis carried out by Evidence Ltd for this project reveals that there has been a fourfold increase in China's collaborative authorship of research papers over the past ten years. The UK is the third most popular partner for China (with 1561 co-authored papers in 2005), after Japan (with 2222 papers) and the US (with 5791). Taken together, EU member states account for almost as many papers as the US (4568). Table 6 shows how these patterns have changed over time.

Table 6 Changing patterns of co-authored publications

Output	1996	1999	2002	2005
China – total papers	15,218	23,174	33,867	59,543
China – collaborative papers	4489	7413	10,840	17,751
US	1364	2104	3267	5791
European Union	1320	2068	2881	4568
UK	430	646	895	1561
Germany	429	615	949	1381
France	213	294	441	827
Canada	294	402	566	1109
Australia	180	353	593	974
Japan	530	945	1461	2222
Singapore	75	204	359	726
South Korea	108	177	342	646

Source: Growth of research collaboration between China and other research orientated economies. Data sourced from Thomson Scientific® and analysed by Evidence Ltd, *Patterns of International Collaboration: China's growing research collaboration* (Leeds: Evidence Ltd, Dec 2006).

Looked at from the UK side, China is now the twelfth most frequent collaborator. This is up from twenty-third in 1997, which makes China the fastest-rising collaborator of the UK, although in total numbers it still only accounts for 4.1 per cent of the UK's co-authored papers. As table 7 shows, these figures need to be set in the context of an overall rise in non-UK co-authorship.

Table 7 UK publication and co-authorship

	1997	2004
UK research publications in journals indexed by Thomson Scientific	96,956	104,219
Papers with a non-UK co-author	17,935	33,411
Collaboration as a percentage of UK output	18.5	32.1

Source: UK international collaboration. Data sourced from Thomson Scientific® and analysed by Evidence Ltd (from J Adams and J Wilsdon, 'A new geography for research collaboration', *Research Fortnight*, 27 Sep 2006).

Aiming higher?
Despite these signs of growing collaboration, there is no room for complacency. The UK has much to offer as a potential partner, but certain difficulties arise from a mismatch between the two countries' funding systems. Unlike the UK's bottom-up approach, government in China is heavily involved in deciding which institutions get funding and for what areas of work. This means that MOST, provincial and municipal policy-makers and many research institutions themselves are well disposed to large, bilateral programmes (eg joint research centres), and tend to place less value on smaller, researcher-led activities. Inevitably, this puts the UK at a disadvantage compared with countries like France and Germany, which invest more readily in large, top-down projects. Working in this way guarantees political visibility and influence, and brings access to people and resources. As one policy-maker told us: 'Joint centres may not always generate brilliant science. But they do generate spill-over effects and other reputational benefits. They can have a big strategic impact.'[159]

This mismatch also gives rise to a perception of the UK as 'all talk and no action', which we encountered frequently during our interviews across China. The UK is seen as good at organising scientific workshops and exchanges, but weak at following these up with meaningful investment in people and projects. The box below includes a selection of quotes reinforcing this point.

Frankly speaking, the UK needs to invest more. The French offer joint funding, the Germans offer joint funding. But the UK doesn't. There's a lot of discussion about collaboration, but no actual money for projects.
Richard Jiang, Shanghai Municipal Science and Technology Commission[160]

Germany is doing better than the UK in developing scientific links. Germany understands what it is doing, why and how. For example, they have a joint centre with the NSFC – a physical building with earmarked funds for research.
Prof Zihe Rao, director, CAS Institute of Biophysics[161]

We've heard a lot about collaboration with the UK. But we want to know how to do it. Talking about it isn't enough. With the US, we know what we are doing, and there are links that go back many years as a result of all the scholarships and students who have spent time in the US.
Professor Biliang Zhang, Guangzhou Institute of Biomedicine and Health[162]

A warm general relationship with the UK doesn't necessarily flow into scientific collaboration. That kind of diplomatic strategy doesn't count for much in the specialised and highly professionalised world of science.
Senior British diplomat, Beijing[163]

When challenged along these lines, UK policy-makers tend to mount a fairly robust defence of the bottom-up approach. One senior figure in the UK government told us:

There's no scientific case for top-down approaches. As I see it, that's the easy answer. Give £6 million to six universities in the UK, China or India and ask them to work together. But that's a distortion, that's not how scientists work. It may be that the best person to work with is in that institution, or they may be somewhere else. It's easy to end up forcing inappropriate alliances.[164]

He has a point. If we look again at the latest data on co-authorship presented in table 7, one of the most striking conclusions is just how well the UK is doing, despite its lack of top-down schemes. France, for all its joint centres and other *grands projets*, accounts for barely half the number of co-authored papers with China that the UK manages to produce.

But the UK needs to do more than rest on its bibliometric laurels. The choice it faces is more strategic. Relying only on bottom-up alliances – on excellent scientists in the UK choosing to seek out and work with excellent scientists in China – assumes a 'perfect market' in scientific collaboration, and does not take sufficient account of 'market failures'. These failures may derive from a lack of awareness of who in either country is doing the most interesting science; they may flow from cultural or linguistic barriers; or they may be the result of established networks crowding out the space for new ones. For example, if a scientist in Oxford is aware of the work of another scientist in her field in Shanghai, she may still prefer to work with colleagues in the US or Europe with whom she has collaborated before.

If China–UK collaboration is to gather in momentum, new mechanisms and models will be required that can combine the best of the British bottom-up model with the more top-down approach that is favoured by China. Globalisation is not only a matter of opening markets, it is also about opening minds. Policy-makers on both sides need to respect the value and integrity of each other's approach, rather than seek to impose a single solution. There are some positive moves in this direction: the UK government now has agreements with MOST covering collaboration on energy research, e-science and zero emissions coal technology. Yet far more could be done, and in the final chapter we recommend some ways forward.

8 Prognosis
The prospects for cosmopolitan innovation

'Our strategic goal as a nation vis-à-vis China should be to capture potential technological synergies, take advantage of evolving scientific and technological complementarities, and collaborate successfully to push out the frontiers of science and the boundaries of technology for the mutual benefit...
of humankind.'

Denis Simon, provost, Levin Institute, Evidence to Hearing on China's High Technology Development, US–China Economic and Security Review Commission, 21–22 Apr 2005

As China continues its explosive growth, so does the market for speculation about its future. Some see China as an economic miracle that will run and run: Chris Patten, the former governor of Hong Kong, says he now has 'half a shelf of Sino-manic-books, which extrapolate gee-whiz statistics into a future noodle-eating paradise'.[165] Others predict that internal contradictions will soon bring Chinese growth to a juddering halt: Will Hutton argues in a new book that China is 'reaching the limits of the sustainability of its current model, and to extrapolate from the past into the future as if nothing needs to change is a first-order mistake'.[166] In the political realm, some see signs of an orderly move towards democracy,[167] while others argue that any such transition is 'trapped', preventing China from following its East Asian neighbours 'along a neoauthoritarian development path… toward a more open society'.[168] And on the global stage, for every commentator predicting China's gradual absorption and positive influence within the international system,[169] there is another arguing that decades of tension, particularly with the US, are inevitable.[170]

However these trajectories play out, many observers within and outside China would agree with John Thornton's assessment in a recent issue of *Foreign Affairs*:

After 28 years of reform, China faces challenges of an unprecedented scale, complexity, and importance. China has already liberalized its markets, opened up to foreign trade and investment, and become a global economic powerhouse. Now its leaders and people must deal with popular dissatisfaction with local government, environmental degradation, scarce natural resources, an underdeveloped financial system, an inadequate health-care system, a restless rural population, urbanization on a massive scale, and increasing social inequality… What is different now is that the pace of change is accelerating while the ability of the state to manage that change is not keeping pace.[171]

China's investment in science and technology, and its ambitions for a new age of indigenous innovation, are at the centre of its efforts to tackle these problems. The government wants *zizhu chuangxin* to be the title of the next chapter in China's epic story. But will it succeed? Is China now on track to become the world's next science superpower?

What is often lost in the welter of statistics about R&D investment and engineering graduates is a sense of the raw power of the changes that are under way, and the dizzying potential for Chinese science and innovation to head in new and surprising directions. We cannot say with any certainty where things may lead, but such large and sustained investment in innovation, within a system that for a long time suppressed such impulses, seems likely to produce a growing number of extraordinary achievements at the frontiers of science over the next ten or 15 years.

Might the premium being placed on innovation itself heighten the pressure for other forms of social and political reform? Cong Cao, a leading expert on China's scientific elite, suggests that scientists and entrepreneurs are unlikely to become a major force for change: 'The scientists and the intellectuals have actually benefited most from the changes in China over the past decade, so they are unlikely to be the ones to challenge the system.'[172] But China's ability – or failure – to create a more open and creative climate, in which innovation can flourish, may ultimately prove decisive. For example, Indian policy-makers are fond of talking up the 'democratic dividend' as their eventual trump card in the game of global science.

This brings us back to the wider choice confronting China between techno-nationalism and more cosmopolitan forms of innovation. In its 15-year plan, China has mapped out what it wants to achieve in scientific and technological terms. What it has not yet done is to spell out the ends to which it wants to direct these strengthened capabilities. What sort of balance will be struck between a focus inwards – on science and technology as a means of securing China's development – and a turn outwards towards collaborative innovation in pursuit of global challenges?

Different elements of China's innovation system are pushing in different directions. There are nationalist overtones to trophy projects such as human space flight, to ongoing efforts to set technological standards, and even to the phrase 'independent innovation', which features so prominently in the new plan. Yet in other ways China is more open to flows of people, investment and ideas than ever before.

As China moves forward, our argument is that independent innovation (*zizhu chuangxin*) needs to go hand-in-hand with cosmopolitan innovation (*sihaiweijia chuangxin*). This will be to China's advantage: an open, diverse and globally engaged innovation system is far more likely to produce the breakthroughs that China needs. But it will also benefit the wider world, which urgently needs China to direct its technological and creative energies towards shared problems of climate change, poverty and disease.

'Why is China so exciting?' asks Joshua Cooper Ramo in a recent paper for the Foreign Policy Centre. 'The prospect of a billion people beginning to choose their own identities… the power of self-innovation.'[173] Projecting this newness and sense of possibility will, he argues, be crucial to the next stage of China's harmonious rise. China's conversations with the wider world 'should be redolent of change and innovation; they should be frank about the failures of reform and the desperate demand for new ideas'.[174]

China's future cannot be secured simply by advancing its own national system of innovation; instead, it must take its rightful place as a leader in the emerging global system of innovation that is taking shape around it. By facing outwards, China will win over those who fear or misunderstand its scientific and technological ambitions. Mutually reinforcing techno-nationalisms will be avoided.

For its part, the UK must do more to strengthen collaboration with China, and encourage the possibilities of cosmopolitan innovation to take root and grow. Below we end with a summary of the headline strengths and weaknesses of China's innovation system, and a series of recommendations for UK policy-makers.

Strengths

— *Mobilisation of resources*
China has a focused and strategic approach to science and innovation policy, which is being supported by dramatic increases in funding at every level, and in the overall share of GDP devoted to R&D.

— *People power*
With 6.5 million undergraduates and 0.5 million postgraduates studying science, medicine or engineering, China has the world's largest scientific workforce. Its university system, at least at the top end, is now world-class.

— *Paper trail*
China now produces 6.5 per cent of the world's scientific papers, with particular strength in selected fields such as material science and nanoscience, where it now ranks as equal or second only to the US.

— *Enterprise insight*
The new 15-year plan recognises innovation by domestic firms, and commerialisation of academic research as key priorities, and is putting in place policies and programmes to deliver this.

— *Offshore innovation*
More multinational R&D is being located in China and there is a gradual move towards using China for high-value, global-facing research by some of the world's most innovative companies.

— *Homeward bound*
There has been a successful drive to attract scientists and engineers back from the US, Japan and Europe, with many of these 'sea-turtles' now occupying top posts in universities, institutes and foreign R&D labs.

— *Property boom*
Intellectual property rights laws, while weak in the past, are now of international quality and more easily enforced. As a growing number of Chinese firms seek to protect their IP, the system should continue to improve.

— *Perceptions count*
The more Chinese science is seen as 'hot', the more multinationals will invest in R&D, the more sea-turtles will swim home, and the more top students will study science. So while there are still problems in parts of the innovation system, growing predictions of China as a science superpower may become self-fulfilling.

Weaknesses

— *Command and control*
Is it really possible to plan for innovation? Some argue that China's policies are based on a mistaken set of assumptions about the ability of top-down measures to stimulate innovation.

— *Quality threshold*
Overall numbers of science and engineering graduates are enormous, but such figures disguise the dramatic variations in quality within the system. Only the top 50 universities are truly world class. Once you get below the top 100, standards plummet fast.

— *China is spiky*
The capabilities for science and innovation are spread very unevenly across China. The poorest regions are close to sub-Saharan Africa, while leading centres are equivalent to advanced European economies. This may lead to unrest and conflict that derails wider efforts to promote economic and political reform.

— *System failure*
With the exception of a handful of international players (Huawei, Lenovo, Haier etc), Chinese companies invest very little in R&D, or in the application of ideas from the academic science base.

— *Bright sparks*
Publications have risen dramatically, but citations less so. It seems that the quantity of published work is outpacing its quality and originality. Even the top science in China often involves the fresh application of techniques and methods that have been developed by others (eg sequencing of the rice or silkworm genome).

— Culture clash
There is a contrast between increasingly excellent hardware and the lagging software of research cultures. There are still big problems in many parts of the academic system with plagiarism and research misconduct.

— Creative class?
The education system is still based on a lot of rote learning and fails to encourage individual creativity. As a result, the innovative potential of many Chinese scientists – and of the system as a whole – may not be fulfilled.

— Democratic dividends
If there is a link between innovation and a political culture that values openness, diversity and tolerance, then China's long-term potential may be undermined by the absence of formal democracy, censorship of the media, and a lack of diversity within the R&D talent pool.

Recommendations for UK policy-makers

1

Unleash mass collaboration
While China's innovation system is rapidly developing, there is a five- to ten-year window of opportunity to move China–UK collaboration to a new level. Bottom-up approaches have worked well in some respects (particularly in producing joint publications) but there is now a need to combine these with top-down investment and prioritisation. The UK should establish a new £100 million global R&D collaboration fund, designed to support the research councils to develop targeted collaborative programmes with key countries. In the context of continued growth in the UK science budget, this does not have to mean damaging cuts elsewhere. It would allow the UK to be more strategic while staying true to the spirit of the Haldane principle (the idea that funding decisions should be made by researchers rather than politicians).

There is no reason why this should compromise research excellence. We may actually get more excellence from targeted links rather than simply allowing the market to deliver bottom-up links as it does now. This could work especially well if we adopt an evidence-based approach and use bibliometrics to identify who is working together productively and then invite them to bid for more resources. But it should also allow support for forms of collaboration which do not necessarily result in publications, especially where these may have wider social benefits, for example collaborative forms of participatory technology development in rural areas.

2

Be a magnet for talent
We need a better understanding of the relationship between migration and innovation. We do not know enough about what AnnaLee Saxenian calls 'brain circulation' between the UK and China. The Office of Science and Innovation, Home Office and NESTA should lead new research in this area.

Scholarships and exchanges will remain critical as a way of strengthening collaborative networks. There are already good schemes in operation such as the Chevening Scholarships and Dorothy Hodgkin Postgraduate Awards, but there is still space for one more focused initiative that can support early to mid-career scientists to build links that they may already have developed to the UK through conferences or short exchanges. Currently, the Royal Society is developing plans for a new scholarship scheme. This should aim to plug the gap between 'talk and action' identified by several of our Chinese interviewees. The new scheme could be branded as the 'Darwin Fellowships' and launched in 2009 (to coincide with the 200th anniversary of Darwin's birth) with 200 places available each year. It should be combined with better alumni management of the schemes that already exist.[175]

At the same time, we need to send more UK scientific talent to China to support two-way flows of people and ideas. This will rely in part on improving general awareness of Chinese science and culture among students in the UK. We should encourage more schools to hire Chinese teachers and teaching assistants, and invest more in Asian studies at university. The decline in Asian studies and language learning in the UK is a worrying trend that must be reversed.

The UK should also aim to become the 'hosts with the most' – the convenor of the world's best scientific conferences, and the facilitator of interactive online spaces where scientists can meet. We should utilise social software and develop the science equivalent of MySpace or Facebook. The journal *Nature* is currently experimenting with this idea, which would build on the UK's position as a centre of science publishing.[176]

Finally, the number of Chinese students in the UK has increased massively over the past five years, but there are already signs that this gold rush may be over. Furthermore, there is anecdotal evidence that the readiness of some UK universities to prioritise income and student numbers over the delivery of quality teaching has damaged the overall reputation of UK higher education in China. University international strategies must now evolve from a commercial model, where maximising numbers is key, to a collaborative model, where research links and joint projects are equally important.

3

Get our story straight
We need to recognise our distinctive assets. As Li Gong of Microsoft said to us: 'China is the world's fastest-growing economy. The US is the home of high-tech and Hollywood. What's the UK's one-line pitch to the world?' We need to better understand and market the UK's strengths in science but also its capacity to combine science with other types of knowledge.

Conventional debates about innovation are still dominated by a 'pipeline' view of basic science flowing into industrial applications. But this model is outdated and in many respects irrelevant to how innovation occurs within the UK economy. It emphasises new products at the expense of services and processes. And it prioritises manufacturing over other areas of innovation such as financial services, the creative industries, retailing, consultancy and the public sector.

At a recent Royal Society meeting, a senior R&D manager from Unilever admitted he would be relaxed if more of their synthetic chemistry moved to Shanghai, because the unique strengths of their British labs were in combining hard science with a sophisticated understanding of what makes consumers tick, drawn from social and behavioural sciences.[177] As innovation becomes more international, the UK's greatest assets may be its openness to international collaboration and its ability to combine advances in basic science with insights from other disciplines, such as psychology, economics, social sciences and law. We will continue to benefit from our own inventions and discoveries, but also from our participation as specialist nodes in global networks of research.

4

Build the knowledge banks
From the 1930s onwards, Joseph Needham pioneered a deep form of engagement with the history and complexities of Chinese science. Today his ongoing project is coordinated by the Needham Research Institute in Cambridge, which is doing excellent work in interpreting the history of Chinese science for the wider world. But given the scale of what is under way in China, the UK needs to invest more in the task of mapping and understanding contemporary developments. It is noticeable that many of the leading experts on these debates (outside China itself) are based in the US.

As well as investing in more academic and policy research, the UK government should expand the Foreign and Commonwealth Office's Science and Innovation Network, so it has the resources to operate beyond the four or five biggest Chinese cities. FCO specialists need more time to gather evidence, create linkages and develop strategy. There is also a need for better coordination between UK agencies on the ground. The proposed opening of a UK research councils office in China is a positive development, providing it is tightly linked to the FCO. One of the tasks of that office should be to monitor the number of UK–China collaborations that flow from bottom-up research. At the moment, there is little accurate data on this. The planned closure of the Department for International Development (DFID) office in China in 2011 is also a missed opportunity. A small, well-focused, ongoing presence could facilitate sharing of UK learning from DFID programmes worldwide about the role of sustainable science and innovation in tackling poverty.

5

Lead global science towards global goals
The UK should be an advocate and exemplar of cosmopolitan innovation in its relations with China. We should initiate a global push to encourage companies to give away or write off unused patent knowledge, which could benefit China, India and the developing world.[178] A particular focus for new UK–China collaboration

1   Z Peng, 'Current status of Gendicine in China: recombinant human Ad-p53 agent for treatment of cancers', *Human Gene Therapy* 16 (Sep 2005); H Jia, 'Controversial Chinese gene-therapy drug entering unfamiliar territory', *Nature Reviews: Drug Discovery* 5 (Apr 2006).
2   'China's war on cancer', *Red Herring*, 24 Apr 2006.
3   Quoted in *Business Week*, 6 Mar 2006.
4   E Callan, 'Cancer drug divides opinion', *Financial Times*, 1 Apr 2005.
5   Organisation for Economic Co-operation and Development, 'China will become the world's second highest investor in R&D by end of 2006, finds OECD', press release, 4 Dec 2006.
6   R Minder, 'Chinese poised to outstrip Europe on R&D', *Financial Times*, 10 Oct 2005.
7   People's Republic of China State Council, *Guidelines for the Medium and Long Term National Science and Technology Development Programme (2006–2020)* (Beijing: PRC State Council, Feb 2006).
8   Hu Jintao, speech, 9 Jan 2006.
9   PRC State Council, *Guidelines for the Medium and Long Term National Science and Technology Development Programme (2006–2020)*.
10 Although the plan itself has since been followed up with a detailed implementation strategy, published in June 2006.
11 D Simon, Evidence to the US–China Economic and Security Review Commission, 21 Apr 2005.
12 RP Suttmeier, Evidence to the US–China Economic and Security Review Commission, 21 Apr 2005.
13 X Guanhua, 'Regarding several big problems in independent innovation', *Keji Ribao*, 6 Apr 2006.
14 Interview with Ze Zhang, 26 May 2006.
15 Y Rao, B Lu and C-L Tsou, 'Chinese science needs a fundamental transformation', and M Poo, 'Big science and small science', *Nature* 432, China Voices supplement, 18 Nov 2004.
16 'Diversionary tactics', editorial, *Nature* 436 (14 Jul 2005).
17 A Segal, presentation at a Tsinghua University innovation conference, May 2006.
18 RP Suttmeier, C Cao and DF Simon, '"Knowledge Innovation" and the Chinese Academy of Sciences', *Science* 312, no 5770 (7 Apr 2006).
19 D Kang and A Segal, 'The siren song of technonationalism', *Far Eastern Economic Review* 169, no 2 (Mar 2006).
20 J Watts, 'China plans first space walk in 2007', *Guardian*, 18 Oct 2005.
21 C Hughes, *Chinese Nationalism in the Global Era* (Abingdon: Routledge, 2006).
22 Chinese Academy of Sciences, 'Pool efforts to build up a national innovation system', press release, 23 Jan 2006.
23 Ministry of Science and Technology, 'Shang Yong: China's indigenous innovation strategy will boost world economy', press release, 8 Aug 2006.
24 National Academy of Sciences, *Rising Above the Gathering Storm: Energizing and employing America for a brighter economic future* (Washington DC: NAS, Oct 2005).
25 J Cooper Ramo, *Brand China* (London: Foreign Policy Centre, 2006).
26 Notably in the pioneering work of Joseph Needham; see J Needham et al, *Science and Civilisation in China*, seven volumes (Cambridge: Cambridge University Press, 1954 onwards).
27 A 'GERD ratio' refers to the amount of government expenditure on R&D.
28 For more on this point, see A Stirling, 'The direction of innovation: a new research and policy agenda?' (unpublished paper, 2005); and M Leach and I Scoones, *The Slow Race: Making technology work for the poor* (London: Demos, 2006).
29 Interview with Ann Clarke, British Library, 16 Oct 2006.
30 Interview with Paul Evans, Elsevier, 9 May 2006.
31 Interview with biotechnology researcher, Sichuan University, 18 Apr 2006.
32 'Nine problems challenge the "innovative state"', *People's Daily*, 9 Jan 2006.
33 DA King, 'The scientific impact of nations', *Nature* 430 (15 Jul 2004).
34 L Leydesdorff and P Zhou, 'Are the contributions of China and Korea upsetting the world system of science?', *Scientometrics* 63, no 3 (2005).
35 R Kostoff, 'The (scientific) wealth of nations', *Scientist* 18, no 18 (2004).
36 X Zhu et al, 'Highly cited research papers and the evaluation of a research university: a case study of Peking University, 1974–2003', *Scientometrics* 60, no 2 (2004).
37 The Chinese Science Citation Index, run by CAS, and the China Scientific and Technical Papers and Citations database, run by the Institute for Scientific and Technical Information of China (ISTIC).
38 S Hebden, 'Open-access research makes a bigger splash', *SciDev.net* (17 May 2006).
39 G de Jonquieres, 'Lies, damn lies and China's economic statistics', *Financial Times*, 22 Nov 2005.
40 CJ Dahlman and J Aubert, *China and the Knowledge Economy* (Washington DC: World Bank, 2001).
41 Remarks at Tsinghua University conference, 'China's innovative capabilities', 21 May 2006.
42 J Kynge, *China Shakes the World* (London: Weidenfeld and Nicolson, 2006).
43 The National High-Technology R&D Program, dubbed '863' because it was launched in March 1986, had invested around US$1.9 billion by 2000 in over 5000 high-tech research projects. It was followed by the National Basic Research Priorities Program, launched in March 1997 and known as '973', which by 2002 had invested US$14.5 million in 60 projects. The Torch Program is a separate initiative, launched in 1988, which aims to develop high-tech industries and development zones. By 2000, it had invested US$3.5 billion in over 2700 projects, many of which are IT-related.

44 Suttmeier, Cao and Simon, '"Knowledge Innovation" and the Chinese Academy of Sciences'.
45 F Jing, 'US$425 million to boost Chinese innovation', *SciDev.net*, 30 May 2006.
46 N Rose, *The Politics of Life Itself: Biomedicine, power and subjectivity in the 21st century* (Princeton: Princeton University Press, 2006).
47 Lux Research, *Sizing Nanotechnology's Value Chain* (New York and San Francisco: Lux Research, 2004).
48 A Hullman, 'Who is winning the global nanorace?', *Nature Nanotechnology* 1, no 81–83 (2006).
49 L Liu and L Zhang, 'Nanotechnology in China – now and in the future', *Nanotechnology Law and Business* (Nov/Dec 2005).
50 C Bai, 'Ascent of nanoscience in China', *Science* 309, no 5731 (1 July 2005).
51 Interview with Professor Chen Wang, 11 Apr 2006.
52 'The future of stem cells: special report', *Financial Times/Scientific American*, July 2005.
53 DTI Global Watch, *Stem Cell Mission to China, Singapore and South Korea* (London: DTI, Jul 2004).
54 Interview with Professor Stephen Minger, 18 Jun 2005.
55 Ibid.
56 All quotes taken from interviews with Li Gong on 18 May 2005 and 26 May 2006.
57 Ministry of Education statistics.
58 A Saxenian, *The New Argonauts: Regional advantage in a global economy* (Cambridge MA: Harvard University Press, 2006).
59 Ibid.
60 Ibid.
61 L Pan, *Sons of the Yellow Emperor: A history of the Chinese diaspora* (New York: Kodansha, 1994).
62 Interview with Deborah Seligsohn, 11 May 2006.
63 Suttmeier, Cao and Simon, '"Knowledge Innovation" and the Chinese Academy of Sciences'.
64 Interview with Jiang Zhu, 26 May 2006.
65 Dinner with returnees, 23 May 2006.
66 Interview with Professor Biliang Zhang, 12 May 2006.
67 Dinner with returnees, 23 May 2006.
68 H Xin, 'Frustrations mount over China's high-priced hunt for trophy professors', *Science* 313, no 5794 (22 Sep 2006).
69 Ibid.
70 Dinner with returnees, 23 May 2006.
71 In 1997, China launched the National 211 Project, which aims to raise 100 of the country's top universities to world-class standards. Within this 100, around 25 are receiving further concentrated investment in particular subjects.
72 'World university rankings', *Times Higher Education Supplement*, Oct 2006.
73 See, for example, recent analysis by Denis Simon and Cong Cao as part of the Levin Institute's project, Global Talent Index™.
74 'The battle for brainpower: a survey of talent', *The Economist*, 7 Oct 2006.
75 D Farrell and A Grant, 'China's looming talent shortage', *McKinsey Quarterly* 4 (2005).
76 Interview with Chongqing S&T Commission, 17 Apr 2006.
77 Kynge, *China Shakes the World*.
78 J Watts, 'Invisible city', *Guardian*, 15 Mar 2006.
79 R Florida, 'The world is spiky', *Atlantic Monthly*, Oct 2005.
80 J Sigurdson, *Technological Superpower China* (Cheltenham: Edward Elgar, 2005).
81 T Li and R Florida, 'Talent, technological innovation and economic growth in China', Richard Florida Creativity Group, Feb 2006.
82 Interview with Shanghai Municipal S&T Commission, 26 Apr 2006.
83 Interview with Sichuan Province S&T Commission, 18 Apr 2006.
84 Interview with Professor Zhang Xingdong, National Engineering Research Centre for Biomaterials, Sichuan University, 18 Apr 2006.
85 R Florida, *The Flight of the Creative Class* (New York: Harper Collins, 2005).
86 Interview with Guangdong Department of Science and Technology, 12 May 2006.
87 INSEAD InnovAsia, 'Dalian, China: The next software outsourcing destination', *Snapshots* (Apr 2006).
88 INSEAD InnovAsia, 'Wuhan, China: Attracting MNCs as an emerging R&D hotspot', *Snapshots* (Mar 2006).
89 A Yeh, 'China lab aims to lead way in research', *Financial Times*, 8 Dec 2005.
90 W Chong, 'China to build 30 new science and technology parks', *SciDev.net*, 19 Apr 2006.
91 Sigurdson, *Technological Superpower China*.
92 R Ferguson and C Olofsson, 'The role of science parks in the support of NTBFS: the entrepreneur's perspective', SLU Ultuna working paper, available at www.ekon.slu.se (accessed 16 Dec 2006).
93 J Lovell, *The Great Wall: China against the world 1000BC–AD2000* (London: Atlantic Books, 2006).
94 All quotes from interviews with Bert van den Bos, 4 Oct 2005 and 15 Nov 2006.

95 Ministry of Commerce, *Report on the Foreign Trade Situation of China* (Beijing: MOC, 2005).
96 S Schwaag Serger, 'China: from shop floor to knowledge factory?' in M Karlsson (ed), *The Internationalization of Corporate R&D* (Stockholm: IPTS, 2006).
97 Interview with Christian Rehtanz, 24 May 2006.
98 Interview with Ralph Lofdahl, 24 May 2006.
99 Interview with Mark Griffin, 23 May 2006.
100 Interview with Ya Cai, 22 May 2006.
101 R Stone and H Xin, 'Novartis invests $100 million in Shanghai', *Science* 314, no 1064 (17 Nov 2006).
102 Interview with Frank Yuan, 25 Apr 2006.
103 Interview with Lan Xue, 12 Apr 2006.
104 J Kynge, *China Shakes the World* (London: Weidenfeld and Nicholson, 2006).
105 Remarks at the Levin Institute/Council on Foreign Relations conference, 'Industrial innovation in China', 24–26 Jul 2006.
106 Interview with Jeff Xiang, 17 May 2006.
107 T Fishman, Evidence to Hearing on China's High Technology Development, US–China Economic and Security Review Commission, 22 Apr 2005.
108 I Harvey, 'West must heed China's rise in the global patent race', *Financial Times*, 21 Sep 2006.
109 Interview with Ian Harvey, 13 Nov 2006.
110 Ibid.
111 Described in R Suttmeier et al, *Standards of Power? Technology, institutions and politics in the development of China's National Standards Strategy* (Washington, DC: National Bureau of Asian Research, 2006).
112 Ibid.
113 Ibid.
114 Ibid.
115 C Cao, 'Chinese science and the "Nobel Prize complex"', *Minerva* 42 (2004).
116 The Fortune Global 500 is a ranking of the top 500 corporations measured by revenue, compiled annually by *Fortune* magazine. In 2006, there were 20 Chinese companies in the list.
117 D Cyranoski, 'Consenting adults not necessarily', *Nature* 435, no 138 (12 May 2005).
118 R Qiu, Presentation at 'The wild east?', Demos/BIOS seminar, London, 9 Nov 2006.
119 Interview with Professor Renzong Qiu, 8 May 2006.
120 Anonymous comment, World Bioethics Congress, Beijing, 6 Aug 2006.
121 Ibid.
122 S Jasanoff, *Designs on Nature* (Princeton, NJ: Princeton University Press, 2005).
123 O Jing, 'Scientific literacy: a new strategic priority for China', *SciDev.net*, 29 Mar 2006.
124 Interview with Professor Renzong Qiu, 8 May 2006.
125 R McGregor, 'Fake chip storm shocks China's scientific elite', *Financial Times*, 15 May 2006.
126 D Yimin, 'Scientists' suicides prompt soul-searching in China', *Science* 311, no 940 (17 Feb 2006).
127 Anonymous interview, PhD biologist, Shanghai.
128 H Xin, 'Scandals shake Chinese science', *Science* 312 (9 Jun 2006).
129 See www.scidev.net/misc/Open_letter.doc (accessed 16 Dec 2006).
130 W Chong, 'China sets up rules to combat scientific misconduct', *SciDev.net*, 10 Nov 2006.
131 See www.xys.org (accessed 16 Dec 2006).
132 Interview with Shi-min Fang, 15 Sep 2006.
133 D Esty and M Porter, 'Ranking national environmental regulation and performance: a leading indicator of future competitiveness?' in *The Global Competitiveness Report 2001–2002* (Oxford: OUP, 2001); R Willis, *A Competitive Environment?* (London: Green Alliance, 2005).
134 Professor Nikolas Rose, Remarks at a BIOS China–EU stem cell workshop, 15 Jun 2006.
135 Brochure from National Chengdu Centre for Safety Evaluation of Drugs, Sichuan.
136 J Lovell, *The Great Wall*.
137 A Peyrefitte, *The Collision of Two Civilisations: The British expedition to China in 1792–4*, tr J Rothschild (London: Harvill, 1993).
138 A Lindahl, *UK–China Partners in Science: Evaluation report* (Beijing: British Embassy, Jun 2006).
139 Technopolis Ltd, *Drivers, Barriers, Benefits and Government Support of UK International Engagement in Science and Innovation* (Brighton: Technopolis, Dec 2005).
140 See, for example, G Roberts, *International Partnerships of Research Excellence: UK–USA academic collaboration* (Oxford: Wolfson College, 2006).
141 Universities UK data, supplied by the Higher Education Statistics Agency.
142 Interview with Caroline Quest, 16 Nov 2006.
143 Speech by Upton van der Vliet, DG Research, at an Atlas of Ideas seminar in Brussels, 7 Dec 2006.
144 'Tsinghua–BP clean energy centre launches in Beijing', *People's Daily*, 23 Jul 2003; J Boxell, 'Surrey satellite becomes China's eye in the sky', *Financial Times*, 27 Oct 2005.
145 For more details see www.ihns.ac.cn/; www.shanghaipasteur.ac.cn/aboutus.html; and www.epsrc.ac.uk/InternationalActivity/Asia/default.htm (all accessed 16 Dec 2006).
146 See www.humboldt-foundation.de/en/programme/index.htm (accessed 16 Dec 2006).

147 See www.mariecurie.org/ (accessed 16 Dec 2006).
148 www.chevening.com/; www.rcuk.ac.uk/hodgkin/default.htm; www.britishcouncil.org/hongkong-education-scholarships-excellence.htm (all accessed 16 Dec 2006).
149 Interview with Jaani Heinonen, 25 Apr 2006.
150 Interview with Georges Papageorgiou, 10 May 2006.
151 Interview with Hartmut Keune, 24 May 2006.
152 For example, for a detailed account of US–China collaboration see RP Suttmeier 'Scientific cooperation and conflict management in the US–China Relations from 1978 to the present' in AL de Cerreno and A Keynan (eds), 'Scientific cooperation, state conflict: the role of scientists in mitigating international discord', *Annals of the New York Academy of Sciences* 866 (1998).
153 'China and India agree joint technology push', News in brief, *Nature* 443 (14 Sep 2006).
154 DA King, 'The scientific impact of nations', *Nature* 430 (15 Jul 2004).
155 Global Science and Innovation Forum, *A Strategy for International Engagement in Research and Development* (London: GSIF, Oct 2006).
156 T Tysome, 'Brits popular but posh', *Times Higher Education Supplement*, 8 Dec 2006.
157 Universities UK data, based on figures from the Higher Education Statistics Agency.
158 Interview with Deborah Seligsohn, US Embassy, Beijing, 11 May 2006.
159 Anonymous interviewee.
160 Interview with Richard Jiang, 26 Apr 2006.
161 Interview with Professor Zihe Rao, 18 May 2005.
162 Interview with Professor Biliang Zhang, 12 May 2006.
163 Anonymous interview with British diplomat, 29 May 2006.
164 Anonymous interview with senior policy-maker, 6 Apr 2006.
165 C Patten, 'Saddled with the worst of both worlds', *Financial Times*, 12 Jun 2006.
166 W Hutton, *The Writing on the Wall: China and the West in the 21st century* (London: Little, Brown, 2007); W Hutton and M Desai, 'Does the future really belong to China?', *Prospect*, Jan 2007.
167 B Gilley, *China's Democratic Future* (New York: Columbia University Press, 2004).
168 M Pei, *China's Trapped Transition: The limits of developmental autocracy* (Cambridge, MA: Harvard University Press, 2006).
169 J Cooper Ramo, *The Beijing Consensus* (London: Foreign Policy Centre, 2004).
170 M Jacques, 'Cold war, take two', *Guardian*, 18 Jun 2005.
171 JL Thornton, 'China's leadership gap', *Foreign Affairs* 85, no 6 (2006).
172 Interview with Cong Cao, 25 May 2006.
173 J Cooper Ramo, *Brand China* (London: Foreign Policy Centre, 2006).
174 Ibid.
175 This is an issue that the Office of Science and Innovation and the Royal Society are already exploring.
176 See http://scratchpad.wikia.com/wiki/Nature_Network_London_Consultation (accessed 18 Dec 2006).
177 Meeting of the R&D Society at the Royal Society, 17 Oct 2006.
178 As with the OneWorld Health project; see www.oneworldhealth.org/

This pamphlet forms part of The Atlas of Ideas project. For more details and copies of our other reports, visit www.atlasofideas.org. We are very grateful to all our funders and their representatives on the project steering group. Particular thanks to Fiona Clouder Richards and Richard Jones of the Foreign and Commonwealth Office and to Lord Sainsbury for their encouragement in the early stages of the project.

Our fieldwork in China would not have been possible without the huge amount of advice and practical support that we received from the FCO's science and innovation team in Beijing, Chongqing, Guangzhou and Shanghai. Many thanks to Nigel Birch, David Concar, Katy Fu, Cai Jing, King Kong, Grace Lang, Anna Lindahl, Robin Porter, Du Ying, Adee Zai, Rapela Zaman and Bronte Zhang.

Thanks also to the Chinese Embassy in London; to Robin Rickard and Jeff Streeter of the British Council; to Jeanne-Marie Gescher and colleagues at CGA in Beijing; and to Jonathan Adams and his team at Evidence Ltd for their bibliometric analysis.

We are grateful to Thomas Harrison for funding an initial trip to China as part of the Norfolk Trust Fellowship programme. Above all, we are indebted to our 140 interviewees for generously sharing their time, insights and opinions. They are too many to name here, but we would especially like to acknowledge the contributions of: Ya Cai, Cong Cao, Guoping Cao, Fu Congbin, Li Gong, Wolfgang Hennig, Jia Hepeng, Ashley Ibbett, Jin Kewen, Sir David King, Xue Lan, Xu Lingyun, Ralph Lofdahl, Richie Lu, Sir Keith O'Nions, Fusheng Pan, Renzong Qiu, Christian Rehtanz, Chen Rong, Lord Sainsbury, Adam Segal, Keith Sequeira, Sylvia Schwaag Serger, Robert Thornes, Bert van den Bos, Eric van Kooij, Jeff Xiang, Jeromy Xue, Jimmy Wang, Frank Yuan, Biliang Zhang, Xingdong Zhang and Ze Zhang.

Finally, at Demos, thanks to Charlie Leadbeater, Kirsten Bound, Molly Webb, Paul Miller and Anna Maybank for the enormous collective effort that has gone into the Atlas project over the past 18 months; to Jenny Wong for research support in the early stages; to Julie Pickard for her skilful copy-editing; and to Tom Bentley, Grahame Broadbelt and Catherine Fieschi for guidance when it was most needed. Any errors and omissions in this report remain our own. The views expressed are those of the authors and do not necessarily reflect those of our project funders.

James Wilsdon and **James Keeley**
January 2007

69 List of organisations interviewed

In China
— ABB Beijing R&D Centre
— Bao'an Middle School, Shenzhen
— Beijing University of Chemical Technology
— Beijing University of Technology
— British Consulate, Guangzhou
— British Council, Beijing and Shanghai
— British Embassy, Beijing
— China Research Institute for Science Popularization
— Chinese Academy of Science (CAS) Institute of Atmospheric Physics
— CAS Institute of Biophysics
— CAS Institute of Microbiology
— CAS Institute of Policy and Management
— Chinese Academy of Social Sciences (CASS)
— CASS Institute of Philosophy
— China Association for Science and Technology
— Chongqing Chongyou IT Company
— Chongqing Science and Technology Commission
— Chongqing University, Faculty of Urban Construction
— Claydon Gescher Associates
— Corning China
— Elsevier S&T
— Embassy of Sweden, Beijing
— Embassy of Switzerland, Beijing
— Ericsson Radio Network R&D Center
— European Commission, Beijing
— German Embassy, Beijing
— Guangzhou Biotechnology Center
— Guangzhou Institute of Biomedicine and Health
— Guangzhou CAS Institute of Energy Conversion
— Guangzhou Municipal Science and Technology Bureau
— Guangdong Province Department of Science and Technology
— Guangdong University of Technology
— Huawei Technologies
— Hutchison Whampoa Guangzhou Baiyunshan
— Institut Pasteur of Shanghai
— Institute of Engineering and Technology, Beijing Office
— Institute of Scientific and Technical Information of China
— Intel
— Kanghong Pharmaceutical Group
— McKinsey and Company, Shanghai
— Microsoft Research Asia
— Microsoft Windows Live
— Ministry of Science and Technology (MOST)
— MOST Department of Policy, Regulation and Reform
— MOST Innovation Fund for Small Technology-based Firms
— National Centre for Nanoscience and Technology
— National Chinese Medicine Safety Assessment and Evaluation Centre
— National Engineering Research Centre for Biomaterials, Sichuan University
— National Natural Science Foundation of China (NSFC)
— Netac
— Nottingham Ningbo University
— Oriental Sun Technology
— Peking University, Department of Economics
— Rolls Royce, China
— Royal Netherlands Embassy, Beijing
— SciDev.net
— Scottish Development International
— Shanghai Ambrosia Pharmaceutical Company
— Shanghai Developmental Biology Research Centre
— Shanghai Genon Bioengineering Co Ltd
— Shanghai Institutes for Biological Sciences
— Shanghai Jiao Tong University, Antai School of Management
— Shenzhen Bureau of Science, Technology & Information
— Shenzhen High-Tech Industrial Park (SHIP)
— Sibionio Genetech
— Sichuan Province Science & Technology Commission
— Sichuan University, Life Sciences College
— Silkworm and Biotechnology Institute
— South China Agricultural University
— Southwest University
— State Key Lab of Biotherapy, Sichuan University
— Sun Microsystems
— Sun Yatsen University
— Tekes, Finland–China Innovation Center
— Tsinghua Science Park
— Tsinghua University, School of Economics and Management
— Tsinghua University, School of Public Policy and Management
— Tsinghua University Graduate School, Shenzhen
— Tsinghua–BP Clean Energy Research and Education Centre
— United States Embassy, Beijing
— Unilever
— Vodafone

In UK, Europe and the US
— China Britain Business Council
— Council on Foreign Relations
— Department for International Development, UK
— East of England Development Agency
— Embassy of the People's Republic of China, London
— European Commission
— Foreign and Commonwealth Office
— HM Treasury, UK
— Intellectual Property Institute
— International Office, Lancaster University
— King's College London, Wolfson Centre for Age-Related Diseases
— Levin Institute, State University of New York
— Medical Research Council
— Office of Science and Innovation, UK
— Queen Mary, University of London
— The Royal Society
— Scottish Enterprise
— Sitra, Finland
— UK Trade and Investment
— University of Cambridge